POLITICAL ORGANIZATION
OF THE PLAINS INDIANS

AMS PRESS

NEW YORK

Library of Congress Cataloging in Publication Data

Smith, Maurice Greer.
  Political organization of the Plains Indians, with special
reference to the council.

  Reprint of the 1924 ed. published by Unitersity of Nebraska
Nebraska, Lincoln, which was issued as v. 24, nos. 1-2,
of its University studies.
  Bibliography: p.
  1. Indians of North America—Great Plains—Tribal
government. I. Title. II. Series: Nebraska. University
of Nebraska studies; v. 24, nos. 1-2.
E78.G73S64   1978   978'.004'97   76-43837
ISBN 0-404-15691-6

First AMS edition published in 1978.

Reprinted from the edition of 1924, Lincoln, Nebraska,
from an original in the collections of the University of
Chicago Library. [Trim size and text area of the original
have been mantained.]

MANUFACTURED
IN THE UNITED STATES OF AMERICA

NT

VOL. XXIV   JANUARY-APRIL, 1924   NOS. 1-2

UNIVERSITY STUDIES

PUBLISHED BY THE UNIVERSITY OF NEBRASKA

CONTENTS

LINCOLN, NEBRASKA

TABLE OF CONTENTS

PREFACE

Next to sociological field work, . . . there are within this branch of study no other investigations so urgently needed as monographs on some definite class of social phenomena or institutions among a certain group of related tribes. A comparative treatment of some social institution as it exists throughout the uncivilized races of the world undoubtedly has value. . . . But at the same time a comparative study suffers from defects which seem wellnigh inseparable from the prosecution of so great a task. A social institution is not an isolated phenomenon, but is. closely connected with a variety of facts. It is largely influenced by local conditions, by the physical environment, by the circumstances in which the people in question live, by its habits and mental characteristics. All these facts can be properly taken into account when the investigation is confined to a single people or one ethnic unity.— Edward Westermarck, in a Prefatory Note to G. C. Wheeler's, "The Tribe and Intertribal Relations in Australia."

The purpose of this essay [1] is to summarize the material available for a study of the political organization of the Plains Indians, with special reference to the council.[2] The sources were meager, since early explorers as well as many field anthropologists slighted or overlooked this phase of the life of the aborigines.

I have presented the facts about the government of each tribe in their proper cultural setting. Details about the council alone, or even of the place of the council in the governing scheme, would not give us a complete view of the subject. All the aspects of government — chieftainship, the executive force, the province of law, etc.— were interrelated with the council. There was a great number

---

[1] In substantially its present form this essay was submitted in 1923 as a thesis in Social Anthropology in partial fulfillment of the requirements for the degree of Master of Arts.

[2] What Dr. Kroeber said of California ethnology was true of the Plains region: "The subject of political organization is perhaps the topic in most urgent need of investigation in the whole field of California ethnology." (1922 b, 285.)

of tribal groups in the Plains area. This fact, which is an aid in the study of certain generally diffused local cultural traits,[3] made for diversity in political organization.

I am under obligation to many persons for kindnesses — to the following for aid in securing books: Mr. M. G. Wyer, Librarian, the University of Nebraska; Mrs. C. S. Paine, Librarian, Nebraska Historical Society; and Mr. A. E. Sheldon, Secretary, Nebraska Historical Society; to Mr. and Mrs. Paul Greer for their encouragement of my work in anthropology; and, above all, to my teacher, Professor Hutton Webster, who suggested this study, for help and criticism.

---

[3] Wissler, 1916, viii.

UNIVERSITY STUDIES

VOL. XXIV   JANUARY-APRIL, 192   NOS. 1-2

I

THE PLAINS INDIANS

Strictly speaking, the Plains Indians were not a unit in any respect. They presented wide differences in physical makeup,[1] language, material life, social organization and religious development. But these tribal or stock types were variants of what was a distinct culture, correlated with the distribution of the buffalo, which grew up in this region.[2] Much of the culture was exotic, but this area of characterization, as it were, molded together heterogeneous elements into a more or less common type.[3]

These Indians inhabited and ranged over a territory broader than the physiographic area which serves to designate them.[4] They were distributed in the region from close to the Rio Grande to the Saskatchewan; and from the Rocky Mountains to Lake Winnipeg, the Missouri and the Mississippi Rivers. Almost all of the limits of the buffalo range (as of 1800) were included in their habitat.[5] Six linguistic stocks were represented in the Plains area proper: the Siouan (the largest), the Algonkian, Caddoan,

---

[1] Dixon, "The Racial History of Man," New York (1923), 423, 426–433; Wissler, 1920, ch. 6.

[2] Wissler, 1907; 1913a; 1917a; and 1920; Kroeber, 1922a. 11; Cf. Anthroplogical Papers, American Museum of Natural History, passim.

[3] Wissler, 1907, 39–40; 1920, 12. Cf. Sapir's remarks on the correlation between the racial and linguistic elements (10).

[4] Wissler, opera cit.; Smith, 368–369.

[5] See Wissler, 1920, 13 for a map of the distribution of the buffalo at the beginning of the nineteenth century.

Athapascan, Shoshonean and Kiowan. Some thirty tribes made up the stocks.[6] Holmes, the veteran archaeologist, has thus characterized the region: [7]

> Traces of the typical culture of the agricultural mound-building peoples of the Mississippi Valley fade out gradually as we traverse the great plains which extend westward to the Rocky Mountains. The region is not well suited to primitive agriculture, and, abounding in game, it encouraged a nomadic rather than a sedentary life, although several stocks . . . claimed and permanently occupied somewhat definite areas. Agriculture was practiced in a limited way in some of the more easterly valleys . . . The population was sparse, the activities were restricted, and as a consequence the varieties of well specialized artifacts were limited in number . . . Pottery, the safest index of the stable status of a people, is somewhat rare in the area, except in the more easterly valleys, and where found is of the simplest culinary type.

We find a key to the description of the Plains culture area in the buffalo.[8] This animal was the center of a culture complex whose ramifications pervaded the entire life of these people. It was the great staple food, even among the semi-agricultural tribes; and many of its by-products were used to good purposes. The regular hunts brought together the bands of the tribes, which usually dwelt in different parts of the tribal range. It played a rôle, too, in religion, in its significance for ritual and worship, and as a guardian spirit.

Other cultural characteristics were: [9] the importance of the horse, the use of the skin tent (tipi), the camp circle

---

[6] Thirty-one, according to Wissler, 1917, 206; thirty-two, according to the same writer. 1916, viii.

[7] Pp. 110–111. Cf. Wissler, 1917, 254 ff.

[8] Paget, 68; McGee, 173; Wissler, 1907, 39–40; 1917a, 206; 1920, 21 ff.

[9] Wissler, 1920, 18.

for formal gatherings,[10] the societies and soldier police,[11] the ceremonially organized sun dance, and a highly developed sign language.[12] Among the typical Plains tribes, agriculture was absent, as were pottery and weaving, and there was but a limited use of roots and berries.

Though the buffalo set the form, it was the horse which intensified and diffused the culture that had arisen in the plains, and increased predatory warfare and periodic ranging.[13] In many instances it made possible the type, since several of the typical tribes had not reached their historic ranges before they acquired the horse (once it was introduced by the Spaniards and other Europeans).[14] Beginning its northward progress from the tribes below the Platte about 1682, the horse reached the Saskatchewan by 1751.[15] Wissler concludes that " while no important Plains traits except those directly associated with the horse seem to have come into existence, the horse is largely responsible for such modifications and realignments as give us the typical Plains culture of the nineteenth century, or which differentiate it from the subtypes in the same area." [16]

By making use of the buffalo as an index of culture, we may group the Plains Indians into three divisions: the

---

[10] " We have seen in the Blackfoot system the suggestion that the band circle organization is in function a political and ceremonial adjunct and that the exogamous aspects of these bands were accidental. So far as we know this holds to a degree for other tribes using the band circle." Wissler, 1911, 4. Cf. Handbook, 1:197.

[11] Wissler, 1916 b, 87 ff; Lowie, 1916, 910.

[12] Clark.

[13] Wissler, 1914; McGee, 173; Grinnell, 1900, 231. "Unfortunately we have no information as to the ethnic conditions in this area before the introduction of the horse and can only assume from certain remote and obscure hints that this was one of the chief factors in the development." Wissler, 1907, 45.

[14] Wissler, 1914, 17.

[15] Ibid., 6.

[16] Ibid., 17.

typical roving, hunting tribes, the eastern semi-agricultural
tribes of the Missouri River, and the western tribes who
inhabited the plateaus and the borders of the Rocky Mountain region.

The most important roving tribes were the Assiniboine,
Blackfoot, Gros Ventre, Crow, Teton-Dakota, Arapaho,
Cheyenne and Kiowa.[17] With them should be classed the
Plains-Cree, Plains-Ojibway, Sarsi and Kiowa-Apache.
All ranged, usually, north and south across the plains and,
though claiming definite territory, hunted in other local-
ities. The characteristic cultural items were strikingly
associated among these tribes.[18] Except for a little tobacco grown for ceremonial purposes, and some feeble
attempts at the cultivation of maize, they did not till the
soil.[19] They had few really permanent encampments.[20]

All of the eastern group [21] were semi-agricultural and
semi-sedentary.[22] They cultivated maize, beans, squashes,

---

[17] Typical, in this connection, means, of course, having the greatest number of traits which are found generally in this area, or having
a majority of them in some heightened degree of association. In
writing of the material culture of the Blackfoot, Wissler com-
ments on "the almost overwhelming similarity of material traits
throughout the Missouri-Saskatchewan area in which this tribe re-
sides." (1910, 166).

[18] " A type of culture, we should note, is the conception of an
associated group of traits, and it is the manner of their association
rather than the identity of the traits that determines it." Wissler,
1914, 17.

[19] Wissler, 1920, 29–30.

[20] Wissler, 1921, v.

[21] The Village Indians included (grouped by linguistic stocks):
Siouan; Hidatsa, Iowa, Kansas, Mandan, Missouri, Omaha, Osage,
Oto, Ponca and Eastern (Santee) Dakota. Caddoan; Arikara, Paw-
nee and Wichita.

[22] Gilmore; Will and Hyde, 59–69; Wissler, 1907, 41; 1913a, 439;
1920, 29–30, Kroeber, 1917, 393: " In the buffalo covered prairies,
agriculture was carried on nearly to the westward limits of profit-
ableness, and that even after the introduction of the horse had
rendered the buffalo one of the most dependably abundant food
supplies in the world."

pumpkins and tobacco, and they used wild plants and roots. Yet they depended in large measure for food upon the hunt. They lived a great part of the year in villages of bark, mat or, more frequently, earth-covered lodges.[23] They made crude pottery. They were representative of a culture intermediate between that of their neighbors to the west and the sedentary agriculturists east of the Missouri and the Mississippi. There was in this region, in fact, a double culture, since the dependence upon the buffalo was clearly an acquisition and a superimposition upon a previous agricultural life.[24]

On the plateaus to the west of the typical tribes lived the Shoshone, the Bannock, the Nez Percé, the Ute and the Kutenai, who were transitional between the Plains and Pacific cultures.[25] These tribes often made hunting trips to the plains east of the mountains in search of the buffalo. Their new experiences and contacts led to their adoption of various Plains characteristics. They did not practice agriculture, but they made use of roots, fish and small game as food: the buffalo supplemented these. They borrowed extensively from the east in ceremonial as well as political organization, though their main affiliations were with their western relatives and neighbors.

Other border tribes,[26] such as the Flathead, to the north,

---

[23] Bushnell.

[24] Wissler, 1907, 42.

[25] Lewis, 179 ff; Kroeber, 1923, 16; Wissler, 1907, 42–43; 1917a, 209–211; Lowie, 1923, 156.

[26] Wissler would put all such doubtful cases in other culture areas (1920, 20); but in order to indicate the cultural relations of the Plains tribes I have included some of them in this study.

the Jicarilla Apache,[27] to the south, and various related tribes of the Caddoan Wichita, to the southeast, assumed certain of the Plains traits.

Save from archaeology and myth and legend,[28] we know little concerning these Indians prior to the period of discovery and exploration. But it is clear that their culture is of comparatively recent origin, and that many of the tribes are late comers to their historic ranges.[29] The culture type was so remarkably adapted to its environment that it is almost certain that it developed within it.[30] One should not, however, underestimate the importance of the influence of the southwest,[31] nor, even, of the semi-agricultural east from which so many groups came. No one tribe can, of course, be said to have originated all of the characteristic traits. " There seems to have been a constant giving and taking until the whole area reached a general level of uniformity. . . . " [32]

Even our incomplete data indicate a great amount of borrowing within the Plains area,[33] a region indeed favorable to the diffusion of cultural traits. The horse was a salient factor in this process. But peaceful penetration of ideas, as well as the roving life, and the many war and hunting expeditions, aided acculturation. Friendships,

---

[27] For example, Goddard says of the Jicarilla Apache, a southern Athapascan tribe related to the Kiowa-Apache: " The method of life of the Jicarilla seems to have been very similar to that of the Plains Indians. They used skin tipis and depended upon buffalo and smaller game for their food supply. They seem to have planted corn only to a limited extent " (1911, 7).

[28] On the value and use of myth, tradition, and legend in sociological studies, see Sapir, 6–8, and Boas, 31 R.B.A.E, 393 ff.

[29] Wissler, 1907, 44–5; 1920, 156; Swanton and Dixon, 12 ff. Cf. qualification of this statement, Wissler, 1920, 151.

[30] Wissler, 1920, 156; 1913a, 442.

[31] Kroeber, 1922a, 11.

[32] Wissler, 1907, 49.

[33] Wissler, 1907; 1917b; 1920, 157; 1910, 166, 169.

alliances and confederations brought tribes together. Proximity, expediency and necessity led to contacts which crossed linguistic and tribal lines. Between 1750 and 1840 the Blackfoot, Sarsi and Gros Ventre; the Assiniboine, Plains-Cree and Plains-Ojibway; the Cheyenne, Arapaho, Kiowa and Comanche; and the Mandan, Hidatsa and Crow were severally members of friendly groups.[34] The Arikara brought their southern culture to the northern village area.[35] The Siouan tribes, especially the Dakotan group, spread over a large territory. The Gros Ventre were intermediaries between two groups of roving tribes;[36] and the northern Cheyenne passed back and forth between the southern hunters and the Teton-Dakota and Mandan.[37]

In Plains Indian sociology the prevalence and significance of societies is to be emphasized.[38] These were of two kinds: ungraded or age-graded. Lowie, who traces the origin of the latter form to the Village tribes, holds that they are a development from an earlier system of ungraded societies, based on natural age divisions.[39] While their organization was ceremonial, they had military, civil and religious functions, differing in this respect among the various tribes.[40] They performed important social functions, the chief of which were the police duties given certain organi-

---

[34] Wissler, 1907, 50.

[35] Lowie, 1912 b.

[36] Wissler, 1907, 50; Lowie, 1916, 954.

[37] Wissler, 1907, 51.

[38] Fully studied in "Societies of the Plains Indians," volume 11, Anthropological Papers, American Museum of Natural History. Cf. the earlier paper by Kroeber (1907a).

[39] 1916, 954. Cf. Kroeber, 1907a, 57.

[40] " It is possible that we shall never be able to say positively that this system is primarily either civil, military or religious and that its other functions are subsequent and subsidiary developments; for there must nearly from the beginning of its existence have been more or less intermingling of its various sides and phases." Kroeber, 1907a, 63.

zations during the tribal hunts, and, as we shall see, the
part they played in the government of some tribes.

The so-called sun-dance [41] was the most important tribal
ceremony of these Indians. It existed among all but the
southern and southeastern tribes.[42] " The sun dance of the
Plains Indian tribes is their most striking ceremonial procedure. It is the only one of their many ritualistic com-
plexes that rises to the level of a tribal ceremony. While
we usually think of these Indians as nomadic . . . it is
well to remember that this nomadism was limited, in the
main, to the summer months. . . . During the winter
season it was the rule that these tribes separated into their
constituent bands and went into permanent winter quar-
ters. The camping places were more or less fixed, generally along a stream, amongst the trees and brush. . . .
Here they eked out an existence as best they could until
summer returned when, in conformity to a previous understanding, the bands of each tribe came together and went
upon a grand hunt. Then food was plenty, feasting and
social activities became the rule. . . . It is in the nature
of things that such a grand picnic should culminate in a
great ceremony, or religious festival, in which the whole
group might function. This ceremony was the sun
dance." [43]

---

[41] The sun dance, so designated, primarily, from the Dakota ceremony, a principal feature of which was sun-gaze-dancing, was an
occasion for supplication of the supernatural powers. Usually in-
itiated by a man or woman in fulfillment of a vow made at some time
of distress, it was the occasion for fasting, religious piety, almost
hypnotic dances, and various tortures, lasting several days. For a
description of a generalized sun dance, see Spier, 461, 462. The
Arapho and Cheyenne, especially the former, are regarded as the
distribution center of the dance and its complex. Spier, 500–520.

[42] Volume 16 of the Anthropological Papers, American Museum of
Natural History, is a thorough study of the characteristics, distribution and origin of this ceremonial feature.

[43] Wissler, 1921, v. Cf. Spier, 505.

A very loose tribe was the unit of political organization. As commonly defined, a tribe is a group characterized by a special name, a distinct dialect, more or less definite territory, and which is capable of united effort.[44] But, as Wheeler found to be the case in Australia,[45] "the determination of a 'tribe' is to a great extent conventional and schematic. . . . There are two kinds of complications. The first is the existence of 'nations'—that is, aggregates of similar tribes. It is not always easy to tell whether we have here to deal with one large tribe, with its local divisions, or whether we are to consider the lesser groups as true independent 'tribes.' . . . The second complication is of the same kind as the first, only in an opposite direction. . . . Each tribal group is subdivided on a local basis into many smaller groups, each with its own share of territory, while within a tribe there may be considerable variations in the dialect." [46]

---

[44] Wheeler, " The Tribe and Intertribal Relations in Australia," London, 1910, ch. 2; Handbook, 1:498; Goldenweiser, 1915, 371. We shall see how far from universal application were the functions assigned to Indian tribes by Morgan (112 ff.). These included, in addition to those given above, the right to invest sachems and chiefs elected by the gentes; a supreme government consisting of a council of chiefs; the right to depose sachems and chiefs; and the possession of a religious faith and worship. But even the loose organization of the tribe in the Plains was an advance over that of the almost tribeless Pacific coast region. Cf. Kroeber, 1917, 396.

[45] Pp. 20–21.

[46] Cf. Wissler, 1920, 87–88: " Thus, while the Crow recognize several subdivisions, they feel that they are one people and support a council or governing body for the whole. The Blackfoot, on the other hand, are composed of three distinct political divisions, the Piegan, Blood and Blackfoot, with no superior government, yet they feel that they are one people with common interests and since they have a common speech, it is customary to ignore the political units and designate them by the larger term. The Hidatsa . . . have essentially the same language as the Crow, but have many different traits of culture and while conscious of a relationship, do not recognize any political sympathies."

The local group or hunting band was the functional basis of the tribe.[47] The band was not simply a family group, as among the eastern Algonkian,[48] but a larger and more complex organization. It was an economic as much as a political group.[49] Tribal solidarity, when war was not being waged, was rarely expressed in political institutions, except once or twice a year.[50]

There were two kinds of tribes and bands: exogamous and non-exogamous. Linked with the custom of marrying outside the group was the inheritance of membership in it according to a fixed system. If kinship was maternal, the divisions are called clans by American anthropologists, following Morgan; if paternal, gentes. Many of the typical Plains tribes had no such system at all, and there is nothing which indicates any order of priority in the arrangement of maternal and paternal kinship groups among the tribes.[51]

---

[47] Wissler, 1911, 3–5; Goldenweiser, 1915, 372; Lowie, 1920, 387; Wheeler, 23 ff. Wissler has the following discriminating note on the term " band ": " As to the origin of the term band, used so generally by the older writers and traders of this area, we have a suggestion from Keating (379): ' The term *band,* as applied to a herd of buffalo, has almost become technical, being the only one in use in the west. It is derived from the French term *bande.*' We may venture that the use of this term for a head man and his following among the Indians of this area was suggested by the analogy between the two kinds of groups, these old naïve observers not being blinded by sociological preconceptions." (1911, 18n.)

[48] Speck, 1915, 292; and 1918; Wissler, 1917a, 154. Cf. Radin, 184–5.

[49] Wissler, 1911, 20 ff.; 1917a, 154.

[50] Wissler, 1917a, 153.

[51] This is not the place for a discussion of the alleged priority of the clan, the special literature of which is considerable. Lowie has written the latest account for those who question the older view (1920, ch. 4–7); Cf. the earlier papers by Swanton (1905, 1906), which brought together much information about the kinship usages of the Indian tribes. His results were opposed to the theories of Morgan and his followers.

II

The Political Organization

THE BLACKFOOT

Under the general name of Blackfoot were known three Algonkian tribes — the Piegan, Blood and Blackfoot — who ranged in part of the region between the north Missouri and the Saskatchewan Rivers.[52] Though they were not politically united under a single government, they spoke almost the same dialect [53] and regarded themselves as one people. Their cultures were so similar [54] that they have always been regarded as a single tribe. Even before the end of the eighteenth century they had become typical Plains Indians.[55]

Each of the three tribes was composed of bands held together by kinship and friendship ties.[56] Grinnell considers these bands true exogamic gentes; [57] but the political and social functions of the band system were so much more important that exogamy can be regarded as an incidental [58] as well as recent function.[59] The Piegan, the largest tribe,

---

[52] Hale, 1885, 707; McClintock, 1; Grinnell, 1892, 177, 208; Wissler, 1910; 1911. Cf. Maximilian, 23:95.

[53] Wissler, 1911, 8. Cf. Kroeber, 1902, 5.

[54] Wissler, 1910.

[55] Ibid., 7. Grinnell believes that the Blackfoot came from the north and east, about Lesser Slave Lake (1892, 177). Cf. Maclean, 49. Wissler, who in an early paper termed them late arrivals on the plains (1906, 162), minimizes the importance of their previous habitat, saying that, except for remote linguistic evidence, we have no basis for saying they did not always live where they were found by the whites (1910, 166).

[56] Wissler, 1911, 18–22.

[57] 1892, 208–210.

[58] Wissler, 4, 18.

[59] Cf. Grinnell, 208.

had twenty-three bands; the Blood, and the Blackfoot six.[60] "The tribal governments are so associated with the band circles that they exist only potentially until the camps are formed; at other times each band is a law unto itself." [61]

The bands had chiefs; [62] but these did not hold a formal office. They were rather the outstanding persons among an indefinite number of men designated as headmen.[63] The band chiefs rarely acted " without the advice of some head men, as to stand alone would be next to fatal. In tribal assemblies, the head men of the bands usually look to one of these as spokesman, and speak of him as their chief. While the tenure and identity of a head man is thus somewhat vague, his functions are rather definite. He is the guardian and defender of the social order in its broadest sense. . . . Above all, the head men are expected to preserve the peace. Should a dispute arise in which members of their bands are concerned, one or more of them are expected to step in as arbitrators or even as police officials if the occasion demanded. . . . The head men may be appealed to for redress against a fellow member of the band. . . . . In all such functions, they are expected to succeed without resort to violence." [64]

The three tribes had chiefs whose office was more definite,[65] though they were not formally elected. " All the head men of the various tribes come by degrees to unanimity as to who would succeed the living chief, though the matter was rarely discussed in formal council. The

---

[60] According to Grinnell, 24, 13 and 8 gens.

[61] Wissler, 5.

[62] Wissler, 22.

[63] These secured their positions through social, ceremonial and military activity. Grinnell, 219.

[64] Wissler, 23–24.

[65] Ibid., 25; Hale, 1885, 707; Maclean, 57–8; Wilson, E. F., 1887, 188; Grinnell, 1892, 219.

main function of the tribal chief was to call councils, he having some discretion as to who should be invited." [66] "Everything of importance was settled in council.[67] While each band was represented there was no fixed membership; yet the head chief usually invited those in excess of one member for each band. There seems to have been no formal legislation and no provision for voting. In former times, the council was rarely convened except in summer. At the end of the fall hunt, the bands separated for the winter to assemble again in the spring. Even in summer they would often camp in two or three bodies, each one under the leadership of some able-bodied band chief, coming together for the sun dance, at which time only the whole tribal government was in existence.

" The organized men's societies among the Blackfoot were, when in large camps, subject to the orders of the head chief or executive of the council and on such occasions seem to have exercised the functions of the head men of the respective bands. . . . When such camps were formed, the head men of the bands were merged into a council for the whole and the men's societies became their executive and police agents under the direction of the head chief." [68]

Maximilian pointed out that the soldier societies exercised much influence in the councils and government of the tribes.[69] About a dozen age-graded groups made up the All-Comrades, the most important of the societies. Curtis

---

[66] Wissler, 25. Cf. Hale, 707.

[67] For descriptions of deliberations, see: De Smet, 1863, 163; 1905, 1041; Bradbury, 47; McClintock, 160, 185. In many Blackfoot narratives, notes Wissler (1910, 7), it is said that the young men fall to fighting while their elders are discussing inter-tribal peace in the council.

[68] Wissler, 1911, 25. Cf. Grinnell, 1892, 219.

[69] 23: 117. Wissler regarded the police functions of the societies as secondary to the ceremonial. No society had a monopoly of police duty (1913b, 370). Cf. Grinnell, 1892, 219 ff.

thought that "the All-Comrades societies were the dominating factor in the tribal organization, and indeed the power of the head chief depended largely on his co-operation with them. At the tribal council called by the chief, not only the chiefs and the head men, but also the chiefs of the societies were summoned." [70]

THE SARSI

The Sarsi, an eastern Athapascan tribe, once powerful, were reduced to dependence on the northern Blackfoot and were associated with them for many years.[71] They hunted the buffalo in their northern range and lived in the manner of Plains Indians.[72] "They are similar in their political and social organization," said Maclean,[73] "to the Blackfeet, having a head chief over the tribe, and a minor chief over each band. . . . Indeed, in all their social customs they are essentially members of the Blackfoot Confederacy." Men who were generous or who performed certain brave deeds could become chiefs; their duties included the adjudication of some disputes and the arrangement of composition for injuries.[74]

THE PLAINS-OJIBWAY

As Skinner has shown, the Plains-Ojibway "present a perhaps unparalleled example of mixed culture." [75] They came into the region west and north of Lake Superior in very recent times.[76] Even their social organization was

---

[70] Cited, Wissler, 1913b, 370, n.i. Cf. Maclean, 59; E. F. Wilson, 1887, 188.

[71] Handbook, article Sarsi; E. F. Wilson, 1888, 242; Maclean, 12. Goddard, 1907, 354; 1915, 190.

[72] Wilson, 243; Wissler, 1910, 10; Goddard, 1907, 354.

[73] P. 17.

[74] Goddard, 1907, 355; 1915, 215–17.

[75] 1914b, 318.

[76] Skinner, 1914a, 477–478; Handbook, 1:278.

transformed by the change of habitat.[77] The tribe was divided into several local bands, each with a chief; but traces of their former organization appeared in their division into exogamic paternal totemic groups, which crossed the lines of the bands.[78]

" The general council [of each band] was composed of those accredited warriors, or okitcitak, who had achieved one or more of the recognized deeds of valor. . . . These men selected the chief who was a man chosen because of his superior bravery, generosity and wisdom." [79]

The tribal chief held his office " by the superior power of his band or following,[80] or his own personal magnetism and reputation for prowess and wisdom." [81] The band chiefs served as a council to the head chief in a tribal encampment.[82] Though these chiefs were the only officers, the people looked upon brave okitcitak as leaders.[83]

In addition to forming the band councils, the okitcitak maintained order and regulated the hunt.[84] Women could — and did — become members of the soldier-police organization and, therefore, might have exercised a small share in the management of the affairs of the tribe.[85] The number of okitcitak was limited only by the abundance of worthy warriors.[86]

---

[77] Skinner, 1914b, 318. For the social grouping of the Ojibway proper, see Jones, 136–137, and Warren.

[78] Skinner, 1914a, 481. He lists 8 bands and 14–16 gentes.

[79] Ibid., 482.

[80] Cf. however, Skinner, 1914a, 482: " All were unanimous that no one gens was considered more important than another . . . ".

[81] Ibid., 487.

[82] Loc. cit.

[83] Loc. cit.

[84] Ibid., 482.

[85] Ibid., 485.

[86] Ibid., 482.

THE PLAINS-CREE

The Plains-Cree [87] formed one of the great divisions of the Cree, a northern forest-dwelling Algonkian group, who were led into the prairie country by their proximity to the buffalo. Their organization was based on the local bands, each of which had a chief.[88] Maclean said [89] that the chiefs, who had first to be soldiers,[90] were elected. One of the bands was considered the most influential: it occupied the center of the camp circle and its chief was the head chief of the tribe.[91]

In the tribal encampment the soldiers' tent or the tipi of a chief served as a meeting place of the council: the head chief and the band leaders.[92] The council managed the affairs of the tribe.[93] It perhaps served, at times, as a court.[94] Mackenzie described the convocation of the tribe by " the elders " to discuss a declaration of war.[95]

THE ASSINIBOINE

An offshoot from the Yanktonai Dakota, the Assiniboine were associated with the Cree since their separation from the parent stock in the seventeenth century. They settled in the region of the Saskatchewan and Assiniboine Rivers, after migrating to various parts of Canada.

Lowie lists seventeen bands of the tribe. He doubts the assertion of Dorsey [96] that these were exogamous clans.

---

[87] They call themselves " prairie Indians " (Peeso, 51), or " prairie people " (Handbook, 2:206).

[88] There were 11 or 14 of these bands, Skinner, 1914a, 517. Cf. Maclean, 76; Hayden, 237; Handbook, 1:359, 361.

[89] P. 76.

[90] Cf. Skinner, 518.

[91] Ibid., 517–518.

[92] Ibid., 518; Paget, 139.

[93] Paget, 139.

[94] Skinner, 1914c, 86.

[95] P. xcix.

[96] 1897, 222–223.

With these bands scattered over a wide area, there was no effective tribal government except at the time of the hunts or while all were on the march.[97]

Each band had a leader or chief, whose authority was dependent upon personal characteristics.[98] Chieftainship was not hereditary, though one qualification for the position, Dorsey thought,[99] was the possession of a large number of kindred in the tribe or band. Gift-giving was a means of enhancing the popularity of a leader. Unsocial conduct led to the deposition of a head man.

The chiefs were expected by the people to guard their welfare, move and place the camp, plan war and direct defense. The leading chief — that is, he who had the largest number of followers and the greatest reputation — was given the head place, subject, always, to the approval of the governed.[100] It was, however, only through the soldier police, whom he directed, that he exercised any strong executive power. The soldiers, chosen because of their bravery, executed the decisions of the council, made up of the chiefs and distinguished old men.[101] At times, they had a voice in the deliberations. Their lodge, in the center of the camp circle, usually served as a council house. When there were two candidates with almost equal qualifications, the councilors chose the head chief. This body of elders regulated the tribal hunt and ordered the punishment of those who violated its rules.[102]

---

[97] See Lowie, 1909a, 35 ff. for the government of the Assiniboine.

[98] Cf. De Smet, 1905, 1124–25.

[99] P. 223.

[100] Wisdom in council, remarks De Smet (1863, 173), added to the dignity of a chief.

[101] Lowie, 53–54. Cf. Maclean, 26. It is important to note that the Cheyenne say they secured their council system of forty-four chiefs from the Assiniboine. Grinnell, 1923, 1:345–48. Cf. infra. p. 26.

[102] De Smet, 1905, 1028.

THE ARAPAHO

The Arapaho were western Algonkian Indians who inhabited the region about the headwaters of the Arkansas and the Platte Rivers, since they were first known to the whites in the nineteenth century. Though allied to the Cheyenne and living in the same district, their Algonkian dialect was quite distinct, indicating, as Kroeber says,[103] a long separation before their recent association. Legends and traditions point to a previous agricultural life in the Red River Valley of northwestern Minnesota,[104] and Lowie concludes from a study of the Plains age-societies that " the parent stock from which the Arapaho and Gros Ventre have sprung must at one time have been in close cultural contact with the Village (Indian) group." [105]

No traces of clans, gentes or totemic divisions have been found among the Arapaho. Five sub-tribes formerly made up the tribe, which had split into northern and southern divisions even before their confinement on reservations. One of these sub-tribes separated from the main group and became the Atsina, or Gros Ventre (of the prairie). Four bands are said to have existed. " Apparently corresponding to these were the four head chiefs that the Arapaho formerly had. These bands were properly subdivisions of the Hinanaéina [Arapaho proper], and appear to have been local subdivisions. A man belonged to the band in which he was born or with which he lived; sometimes he would change at marriage. When the bands were separate, the people in each camped promiscuously and without order. When the whole tribe was together, it camped in a circle that had an opening to the east. The members of each band then camped in one place in the circle." [106]

[103] 1902, 5. Cf. Mooney, 1896, 954.
[104] Handbook, 1:72. See Kroeber, 3, for the material culture of the Arapaho.
[105] 1916, 954.
[106] Kroeber, 8. Cf. Mooney, 956; Wissler, 1911, 5.

Clark, whose description of the tribe is vague, gave the following account of its government: [107]

> Formerly the head chief of the Arapaho nation was elected by a grand council; this was, however, a mere matter of form, for, as they have said, " The man who had led the soldiers to war, had done many brave things was sure of the election." They also had sub-chiefs, head men of the soldier bands, and frequently a council or peace chief, who, as a rule, held his position by the power of his persuasive eloquence.

But Kroeber thinks that the tribe had no formal principal chief.[108]

> When one of the four head chiefs died, another was chosen from among the dog-company—men about fifty years old, who have performed the fourth of the tribal series of six ceremonials. If a chief was unsatisfactory, he was not respected or obeyed, and so gradually lost his position. Another informant stated that chiefs were not formally elected: the bravest and kindest hearted men became chiefs naturally, but there were no recognized or regular chiefs.

The age societies assumed an important position in the tribal government, if they furnished the chiefs. One of the age societies, the so-called Bitahínena, " performed police duty in camp, when traveling and on the hunt, and were expected to see that the orders of the chief were obeyed by the tribe. For instance, if any person violated the tribal code or failed to attend a general dance or council a part of the Bitahínena was sent to kill his dogs, destroy his tipi or, in extreme cases, to shoot his ponies." [109]

THE GROS VENTRE

Though considered a subtribe by the Arapaho, the Gros Ventre or Atsina led a separate existence for over two

---

107 P. 43.

108 Pp. 8–9.

109 Mooney, 988. According to this writer, the soldier society of the Arapho came from the Cheyenne.

hundred years.[110] During the nineteenth century they were closely associated with the Blackfoot. Their habitat was widely variable, and they have been observed hunting the buffalo in many parts of the great area between the Saskatchewan, the Missouri and the Platte Rivers.[111]

The tribe was divided into eight local groups, which partook, also, of the nature of gentes.[112] Each band had a recognized head chief. " When summer came, the clans [gentes] joined and camped together in the large campcircle. In this, the different bands had definite places." [113] The ceremonial organization of the tribe, based on the age societies, was similar to that of the Arapaho.[114]

THE CHEYENNE

Coming out on the plains from southwestern Minnesota, the Cheyenne adapted their mode of life so completely to the new environment that few traces of their previous sedentary culture remained.[115] Their historic culture was, therefore, recent and almost all borrowed.[116] It was only in tradition that the ancient life of this Algonkian tribe was remembered.[117] Grinnell declares [118] they grew crops until the middle of the nineteenth century; but Mooney, differing with him on this, as on other matters, considered them only hunters.

For a long time the Cheyenne were allied with the Arapaho, a neighboring tribe of the same linguistic stock. The existing division of the tribe into northern and

[110] Kroeber, 1908, 145.
[111] Ibid., 147.
[112] Kroeber, 1902, 8.
[113] Kroeber, 1908, 147.
[114] Ibid., 227. Cf. 230.
[115] Grinnell, 1918.
[116] Mooney, 1907, 361.
[117] Ibid., 361, 420, Grinnell, 1923, 1:247.
[118] 1915, 1; 1918, 375; 1923, 1:247–54.

southern divisions is less than a hundred years old, but the united tribe was itself made up of two tribes. There has been some dispute concerning the social organization of the tribe. Mooney declared that the Cheyenne were made up of ten non-exogamous bands ordered on a ceremonial geographic basis in the camp circle.[119] Grinnell once contended that these sub-groups were exogamous bands,[120] but in his most recent work he modifies this view,[121] admitting that the evidence for the clan system is inconclusive.[122] Descent, he says, was matrilineal and he finds it hard to ignore " the amount of testimony received from a number of old men as to the practice of exogamy in old times." [123]

---

[119] 1907, 410–11. Cf. his statement in Handbook, 1:254: " One authority claims these divisions as true clans, but the testimony is not conclusive. The wandering habit—each band commonly apart from the others, with only one regular tribal reunion in the year— would make it almost impossible to keep up an exogamic system. While it is quite probable that the Cheyenne may have had the clan system in ancient times while still a sedentary people, it is almost as certain that it disappeared so long ago as to be no longer even a memory. The present divisions seem to have had an entirely different genesis, and may represent original village settlements in their old homes . . . " In any event, concludes Wissler (1911, 5), their bands were predominantly conventional, since the actual groups who lived in the various Cheyenne camps did not coincide with the band grouping.

[120] 1905. Grinnell said, in consonance with his understanding of the clan-like organization of the tribe, that " the women exerted great influence in the tribe, and were in old times, and even are now to a great extent, the real rulers of the tribe. They are very often the leading spirits of the family, and their husbands usually follow their advice. It is only the strong women that possess this influence, but of them there are a good many " (1905, 137). Cf. ibid., 1923, 1:128.

[121] 1923, 1:88.

[122] Ibid.,1:91.

[123] Loc. cit.

A council of forty-four chiefs governed the tribe.[124] Members were elected for ten-year terms.[125] Four [126] of these led the governing body and decided matters of minor importance. They were of equal authority.[127] Since the principal chiefs could name their successors, the office can be said to have been in a sense hereditary.[128] Each of the ten bands was represented by four members.[129] Ordinarily, a few old men might attend the meetings of the chiefs.[130] " Of strong influence in the government of the tribe was the sentiment of the soldier bands. These were the police and chief fighting force of the tribe. . . . [They] might at times exercise pressure on the chiefs, and induce the council to act in some particular way that [they] desired." [131] The soldiers enforced the decisions of the council,[132] but it was seldom that the chiefs had not already felt out public opinion.[133]

This council system was received from another Plains tribe about 1750, if we are to believe one Cheyenne tradition.[134] The legend tells how a Cheyenne woman was captured by the Hohe, or Assiniboine, among whom she observed the functioning of their council. When she returned to her own people, she established a similar body of forty-

---

[124] Grinnell, 1:336–44; Mooney, 1907, 402–3; G. A. Dorsey, 1905a, 12 ff. For the functioning of the council, see Grinnell, 1915, 47–8, 61, 85, 97; Mooney, 1896, 818.

[125] Grinnell, 1923, 1:340. There was much ceremony about the election and procedure of the council.

[126] For the reverence paid by the Cheyenne to the mystic number four, see Clark, 103.

[127] Unless they chose to delegate supreme power to one of their number.

[128] Grinnell, 1:340.

[129] Cf. Mooney, 1907, 403, for a contradictory view.

[130] Grinnell, 1:339.

[131] Ibid., 337–8.

[132] Ibid., 336.

[133] Ibid., 339–40.

[134] Grinnell, 1:345–8. Cf. Mooney, 1907, 371.

four of the principal men of the tribe. This ruling body seemed to please the Cheyenne, who thereafter followed the custom. But another short tale says that this political organization was created by the culture hero, "the great Prophet," who chose the first chiefs from the four bands of soldiers.[135]

THE KIOWA

The Kiowa, forming a distinct linguistic stock, had their range in Colorado and Arkansas. Kendall declared their "customs and manners" resembled those of the Comanche.[136] The tribe was divided into two general local divisions, each of which was subdivided. It did not have the clan system.[137] Each division had its own chief, who was subordinate to the head chief of the tribe.[138] One band took the head place in the camp circle and furnished the head chief.

The tribal organization was strongly centralized for such a nomadic group.[139] Mooney thus described their government: [140]

The tribal government was formerly committed to the care of a head chief and the chiefs of the several bands, together with the war chiefs who had control in military affairs. Women had no voice in the government . . . The chiefs in former times . . . must have exercised almost despotic powers and were feared as well as respected by their people . . . Camp and ceremonial regulations were enforced and their violation punished by the Yä' pähe, acting under direction of the war chiefs. Personal grievances were avenged by the injured party or by his relatives, without interference by the tribe.

---

[135] Grinnell, 1:344–5. Cf. Dorsey, 1905a, 3.
[136] 1:213.
[137] Mooney, 1900, 227.
[138] Ibid., 248.
[139] Mooney, 1911, 174.
[140] 1900, 233.

" As the (Kiowa) Apache are practically a part of the Kiowa in everything but language, they need no extended separate notice." [141]

THE COMANCHE

The Comanche were the only Shoshonean Indians who were a typical Plains tribe. They were a branch of the Shoshone proper, who, migrating to the southeast, reached New Mexico and the Panhandle country about 1700.[142] The Comanche never cultivated the soil.[143] Expert horsemen, they fought their way to a position of preëminence among the tribes of the southwestern plains.[144]

The tribe existed in three grand divisions, each of which was subdivided into bands.[145] There was no gentile system.[146] Each band had a chief and a varying number of minor leaders,[147] who were dependent on the support of their followers. There was a head chief of the tribe; but the unifying bond between the roaming groups was the tribal council.[148]

Captain Clark said [149] of the Comanche tribe that " their form of government is about like that of all the Plains Indians. There is no special form of election to the position of chief; public opinion, the sentiment of the camp, elevates those specially distinguished in war to the highest

---

[141] Mooney, 1900, 248.

[142] Clark, 119–20; Thomas James, 114 n. The Shoshone say the Comanche left them to search for horses and game. Cf. Lewis and Clark (T), 6:108.

[143] Marcy, 1854, 96; Burnet, 231; Pike, Appendix II, 17.

[144] Clark, 121; Neighbors, 128. Their language was the trade language of the region. Handbook, 1:328.

[145] Marcy, 1854, 94 ff; 1866, 43 ff; Burnet, 230; Neighbors, 127, 128; Thomas James, 198; The Comanche remember twelve bands, but they probably had more.

[146] Mooney, Handbook, 1:328; 1911, 173.

[147] Burnet, 231; Marcy, loc. cit.

[148] Neighbors, 127, 130; Bancroft, 509–510.

[149] P. 121.

position of power. No council is called for this election, other than that held on the battlefield. Their councils are held, as with other tribes, to discuss matters of importance. No special laws are made, and no special dignity is attached to the office of the camp crier, who promulgates the decision of the council, or the orders of the chief, or imparts general information."

The head chief exercised little power.[150] His followers might depose him for mishaps or defeats which came to the tribe.[151] He was guided by the council of chiefs and old men, who expressed popular opinion. The minor chiefs were ranked according to the number of their followers. They would call councils of their bands when necessary.

When the bands met, they united in the council of the tribe.[152] The sessions were open to the people, though, of course, only the sub-chiefs and a few old, brave warriors had seats.[153]

Meetings were called by the principal chief. "In deliberations in council they consult each other, and one addresses the meeting. The council is opened by passing the council pipe from one to the other, and invoking the Deity to preside. It is conducted with great propriety, and closed in the same manner." [154] Great respect is paid to ancestral customs and precedents. According to Neighbors, apparent unanimity was required for decisions,[155] and, as one writer said, these were " of little moment, unless they meet the approbation of the mass of the people; and for this reason these councils are exceedingly careful not to run counter

[150] Burnet, 231; Neighbors, 130; Clark, 121.
[151] Marcy, 1854, 97.
[152] Bancroft, 509; Neighbors, 127; Marcy, 1866, 43.
[153] Neighbors, 130–31; Thomas James, 121, 203, 224.
[154] Neighbors, 130.
[155] Loc. cit. Cf. Bancroft, 209, where it is stated that the decisions were decided by majority rule.

to the wishes of the poorer but more numerous classes." [156]
Certain judicial functions were exercised by the council.[157]
Its members executed the orders and judgments.[158]

THE FLATHEAD

The Flathead,[159] or Salish Indians, inhabited the western
part of what is now Montana.[160] In sharp contrast to the
complex social organization and the more or less developed
governmental system of the coast Salishean tribes, the
organization of the Flathead was loose and democratic.[161]
This is another of the less advanced American tribes whose
kinship rules were indisputably paternal.[162] Hale [163] and
Wilkes [164] reported that they could hardly be said to have
any regularly organized tribal government, roaming, as
they did, in small bands, which united — and rarely — only
to fight their common enemies, such as the Blackfoot.

---

[156] Cited in Bancroft, 509, note 112.

[157] Ibid., 509, 510; Burnet, 231. Among other functions were,
for example, matters relating to the chieftainship (Clark, 121;
Marcy, 1854, 97), war (Thomas James, 224), the disposal of prisoners (Thomas James, 121; De Smet, 1863, 234), etc.

[158] Marcy, 1854, 97; Bancroft, 510. There was no special police
body in the tribe in connection with the hunt. Lowie, 1915b, 812.

[159] Their popular name does not fit them at all. Cf. Handbook,
2:417.

[160] Wilkes, 446; Hale, 1846, 205–207; Clark, 300; Bancroft, 1:264.
Cf. Hale, 201: " The tribes of the interior depend, in part, for their
clothing on the buffalo skins which they obtain, either by barter or
by hunting. And for both these purposes it is necessary for them
to visit the region near the foot of the Rocky Mountains frequented
by that animal. This, however, does not, except with some of the
Shoshonees, give rise to a general removal of the tribe, but merely
an expedition of the principal men, their families being left, in the
meantime, encamped in some place of safety."

[161] Hill-Tout, 159.

[162] Hill-Tout, 158; Boas, 1889, 829.

[163] P. 207.

[164] P. 447.

Councils of elders in each village commune of the tribe made up the governing bodies, according to Hill-Tout.[165]

The simplest form of social organization is found among the interior hunting tribes, where a state of pure anarchy may be said to have formerly prevailed, each family being a law unto itself and acknowledging no authority save that of its own eldermen. Each local community was composed of a greater or less number of these self-ruling families. There was a kind of headship or nominal authority given to the oldest and wisest of the eldermen in some of the larger communities, where occasion called for it or where circumstances arose in which it became necessary to have a central representative. This led in some centers to the regular appointing of local chiefs or heads whose business it was to look after the material interests of the commune over which they presided; but the office was always strictly elective [166] and hedged with manifold limitations as to authority and privilege. For example, the local chief was not necessarily the head of all undertakings. He would not lead in war or the chase unless he happened to be the best hunter or the bravest and most skillful warrior among them; and he was subject to deposition at a moment's notice if his conduct did not meet with the approval of the elders of the commune. His office or leadership was therefore purely a nominal one.[167]

THE KUTENAI

The Kutenai, a distinct linguistic family, were comparatively recent intruders from the plains area,[168] who settled in the southern part of British Columbia and the northern parts of Idaho and Montana west of the Rocky Mountains.[169] The tribe existed in two groups: the Upper Kutenai (of four bands) and the Lower Kutenai.[170] Hale, an early observer, declared that " in appearance, character

---

165 Pp. 158–9. Cf. Bancroft, 275, 276.

166 Cf. De Smet, 1863, 297.

167 Cf. Hale, 1846, 208; Wilkes, 448.

168 Chamberlain, A. F. 1905, 178; 1892, 550, 575; Hale, 1887, 197. Boas says that the folk tales of the Kutenai, " show intimate relations to the tribes of the plateaus as well as to those of the plains east of the mountains." (1918, 281).

169 Chamberlain, 1905, 178; Bancroft, 1:311.

170 Chamberlain, 1892, 550; 1905, 178; Boas, 1889, 806.

and customs they resemble more the Indians east of the Rocky Mountains than those of Lower Oregon." [171] The Upper Kutenai were essentially a hunting group; [172] the lower division, because of environmental differences, were more fishers and collectors. [173] It is the Upper Kutenai, then, to which writers refer when they mention the tribe as coming regularly across the mountains to hunt the buffalo. [174]

The social structure of the Kutenai was remarkably simple. According to Chamberlain, [175] "there are, apparently, no evidences of the present or past existence among them of clan systems, [176] totemic institutions, [177] or secret societies, etc. Each local or tribal community seems to have had a chief. . . . This office (to be held only by the males who had reached the age of thirty) was hereditary, [178] but the people had always the right to select some other of the family when the heir was incompetent or unworthy, or refused the chiefship. [179] It would seem that the 'medicine men' sometimes influenced the selection.

"The power of the chief was limited by the advice and action of his council. In former days there was also elected a 'buffalo-chief,' whose authority extended over the great hunting expeditions."

The council was made up of the chiefs and head men. "When the chief wished to consult with his people he called them in a loud voice to come to his large tepee. It

---

[171] 1846, 205.
[172] Boas, 1889, 807.
[173] Ibid., 807, 818.
[174] Ibid., 818; Clark, 231. They hunted with the Blackfoot and some other Plains tribes, with whom, evidently, they made alliances, Chamberlain, 1905, 179. Cf. Boas, 1918, 53, number 44.
[175] 1905, 185. Cf. Ibid., 1892, 556–559; Handbook, 1:740.
[176] Cf. Boas, 1888, 238.
[177] Cf. Boas, 1889, 819.
[178] Descent was in the female line. Cf. Chamberlain, 1905, 186.
[179] Cf. Boas, 1889, 836; Bancroft, 275.

is probable that from early times a sort of advisory council existed." [180]   The council may have exercised certain judicial functions. [181]

THE NEZ PERCE'

The culture of the Nez Percé consisted in almost equal proportions of elements common to the Plains Indians and the Pacific coast tribes. [182]   Before the appearance of the horse, however, it was more representative of the west than the east. [183]   The tribe lived in a large area in Idaho and parts of Oregon and Washington.   The Nez Percé formerly made trips over the mountains to the buffalo grounds, where they had many battles with the Shoshone, Crow, Blackfoot and other Plains tribes, [184] but this was only after they acquired the horse. [185]

" The Nez Percé tribe was divided into bands upon the village or geographical basis.   Each village had its chief, its fishing place, and its strip of territory along the river. Several village groups often came together to make up a war-party, but there is little evidence of close relationship in village groups in time of peace." [186]   Chiefs were elected.   There was the common distinction between war and peace chiefs.   Each village had at least one peace chief. War leaders were elected in council.   Hardly ever did a war chief unite the whole tribe under his influence.   The authority of the peace chief was limited to his own village or to his own people while on the march.   In times of peace, the war position was unimportant.   All the chiefs

---

[180] Chamberlain, 1892, 556.

[181] Bancroft, 276.

[182] Spinden, 270.   In point of material culture, says Wissler (1910, 165–66), the Nez Percé showed a greater relation to the Crow and Hidatsa than to the Blackfoot, their more immediate neighbors.

[183] Spinden, 271.

[184] Hale, 1846, 212.

[185] Spinden, 271.

[186] Spinden, 242.

sought to obtain the favor of the populace, since their power depended on their following.[187]

Spinden sketched the council of the tribe.[188]

The council consisted of the chiefs and the old men. There was a village council which helped the chief in administering justice, and a tribal council which met to discuss intervillage matters and affairs of war and peace. These tribal councils might be large or small, comprising a group of villages or the whole tribe [189]. . . . . Whenever two or more large bands met, such councils might be formed to discuss affairs of moment.[190] The rule for decision was perfect agreement, and so the councils were often long drawn out. . . . The rule of the council was unanimity, and this could be effected only by calm reasoning where facts were to be considered, and by impassioned appeal, when the decision depended on sentiment. Often a public speaker or herald, repeated word for word the orations of the chiefs in order that the assembled multitude might hear.

----

[187] Maclean remembered that " the Nez Percé chiefs were a notable class of men, well skilled in all the arts of diplomacy, firm in the exercise of their authority " (38).

[188] Spinden, 243. It was the need of defence against the roving bands of invaders from the Plains which led to the greater unification of the tribe, whose organization had previously been quite loose. " The social structure of the tribe was marked by the simple geographical or village type, without totemic clans, and with a village chief who divided with the shaman whatever autocratic power there was . . . Overlying this village-community form of social organization among the Nez Percés was the tremendous importance of war and the nationalizing office of war-chief. The necessity of united defence against invading war parties from the Plains probably brought about the tribal integrity of the sixty or more independent villages." Spinden, 271.

[189] The council " varied in size according to the importance of matters under discussion and the breadth of the territory involved." Spinden, 244.

[190] " There were also intertribal councils. At these the chiefs met and argued while the pipe was passed around and the listeners sat in a circle. Such intertribal councils were common between the Nez Percé and the Cayuse, Wallawalla, and Yakima, formed to discuss war against the common enemies. Treaties between enemies were also ratified at such councils." Spinden, 243.

There was no regular police, and the chiefs and the council exercised the power of disciplining individuals.[191]

THE SHOSHONE

According to one tradition, the Shoshone Indians were driven from the plains into the mountains and the Utah Basin,[192] but this appears to be in error. They did not practice agriculture, the more advanced living by fishing and hunting, and the less advanced by collecting and fishing.[193] There were many bands in the plateau states; these varied in culture and customs.[194] Some — as the Dog-Eater and the Green River Snakes — were almost typical plains peoples, ranging over the mountains and living primarily on the buffalo.[195] Others — the so-called Digger Shoshone — represent almost the lowest stages of economic development.[196]

The most northerly representatives of the Shoshonean stock, this tribe was related to the Comanche,[197] who were typical Plains Indians. It was, however, most closely connected with the Bannock by proximity, intermarriage, language and customs. For the northern Shoshone, at least, Lowie considers the influence of Plains culture recent, although there were local migrations of bands near the prairie eastward, and that this portion of the tribe had long occupied the plateau region.[198]

---

[191] Spinden, 244.
[192] Schoolcraft, 1:199. Cf. Kroeber, 1907b., 165; Lowie, 1909b, 173, for a contradiction of this view.
[193] Schoolcraft, 1:202; Handbook, 2:557. Cf. Hale, 1846, 201.
[194] Kroeber, 1907b, 113.
[195] Lowie, 171, 184–191.
[196] Bancroft, 440–442; Schoolcraft, 1:202.
[197] Cf. supra.
[198] Lowie, 173. " The mythology of the Shoshone indicates a closer connection with the people of California and the Great Basin than with their eastern neighbors of the Plains." Ibid, 236. " The Wind River Shoshone had at least one institution that clearly cor-

Groups of families were the social units, although villages sometimes existed.[199] When the tribe did collect, a camp circle was formed, as in the Plains region: it was used for councils and dances in times of war and while on tribal hunts.[200]

Lowie says: [201]

From the accounts of early travelers, it is quite clear that the powers of the chiefs were advisory rather than dictatorial.[202] 'Little' chiefs attained their dignity by the performance of warlike deeds, and there were sometimes as many as ten in a single community. The head-chief was general director of the camp, presided at councils, [203] received visitors from other tribes, and conducted hunting and fishing excursions; but beyond this his power rested simply on his personal influence . . . The chief seems to have enjoyed no privileges of any kind. At a dance or hunt, he was assisted by policemen armed with quirts. At Fort Hall, at least, a camp crier announced important occurrences. The head chieftaincy was not hereditary. Sometimes a chief was succeeded by his son; but this was not by any means necessary, nor was it necessarily the oldest son that fell heir to the position . . . Ability as an orator seems to have counted for something in the estimation of a chief.

Neither the chief nor any other member of the tribe exercised judicial functions [204] Murderers were regarded as irresponsible, and were dealt with by the individual family and friends of the victim.

---

responds to a typical feature of the Plains Indian age-societies. Whenever the tribe was on the march or engaged in a communal hunt, two or more bodies of men directed the movements of the people and were invested with special police functions." Lowie, 1915b, 813. See, Kroeber, 1907b, 113, for the Wind River Shoshone.

[199] Lowie, 1909b, 208; Wyeth, 207; Fitzpatrick, 262.
[200] Lowie, 208.
[201] Pp. 208–9.
[202] Cf. Bancroft, 436.
[203] Cf. Lewis and Clark, 2:163; De Smet, 1905, 262.
[204] Cf. Wyeth, 207; Fitzpatrick, 263.

Councils were familiar to the Shoshone,[205] and the mythology of the tribe has references to them.[206]

THE BANNOCK

The Bannock have not always been distinguished from the Shoshone proper, even though their Shoshonean dialect more closely resembles the Ute than any other of their cognates.[207] The two tribes were neighbors for a long time and intermarried considerably. Leonard, who saw them before they acquired the horse, thus described them: [208]

They generally make but one visit to the buffaloe country during the year, where they remain until they jirk as much meat as their females can lug home on their backs. Then they quit the mountains and return to the plains, where they subsist on fish and small game the remainder of the year.

The horse came to them before it reached the Shoshone. Henceforth they entered upon a more nomadic life, which led them to assume some of the characteristics of the Plains Indians. Wyeth noticed the superiority of the Bannock, poor as they were, over their less advanced neighbors.[209]

Five bands made up the tribe; these were grouped in two geographic divisions. Clark asserted that one of their chiefs told him " all their customs, dances, religious ceremonies, implements, ways of living, lodges, laws, punishments etc., were like the Shoshoni." [210] But the loose organization of the Shoshone could hardly have continued unchanged by the transition of the Bannock into a hunting tribe. And it did not, if we are to credit Wyeth's state-

[205] E. M. Wilson tells of councils held by the Wind River Shoshone while he was living among them as a prisoner (20, 112 ff., 205, 206).

[206] Lowie, 247, 274, 291, 293.

[207] Kroeber, 1907b, 115 ff; Handbook, 1:129; Clark, 60.

[208] P. 148.

[209] Pp. 206, 208.

[210] P. 60. Cf. Handbook, 1:129.

ment that the horse and the hunting life "caused an organization among the Bonacks, which continues the year through, because the interests which produce it continue; and it is more advanced than that of the other Snakes." [211] Johnston, another contributor to Schoolcraft's "History," gives us two facts of interest: that disputes concerning women were usually settled, before the white officials came, by the chiefs;[212] and that the bands had council houses.[213]

THE UTE

The Ute Indians lived in the richer game parts of Utah and adjacent states, roaming over a wide area.[214] Nonagricultural, they depended, to a much larger degree than did their cognates, upon hunting.[215] There were seven Ute tribes (bands) in what is now Utah.[216]

We know almost nothing of the social organization of the tribe.[217] At one time the seven tribes were united, temporarily, in a confederacy. The southern Ute preserved remnants of what may have been a clan organization.[218] The bravest warriors in the bands were chosen chiefs by the principal men.[219] But the chiefs wielded little power.[220] There was no soldier band.[221] Families acted together, when necessary for certain enterprises. Miss Densmore noted a council of war,[222] and Lowie the

---

[211] P. 208.

[212] P. 224.

[213] Ibid., 223.

[214] Handbook, 2:619, 875; Bancroft, 464; Chamberlain, R. V., 1909, 27.

[215] Chamberlain, R. V., 1911, 335–36.

[216] Handbook, articles, Ute, Southern Ute.

[217] Densmore, 1922, 24; Handbook, 2:874.

[218] Hrdlička, in Handbook, 2:619.

[219] Clark, 390.

[220] Dodge, 74.

[221] Clark, 390.

[222] P. 147.

council of election, by the group, of the leader of the Bear Dance ceremony.[223]

THE DAKOTA

The great Dakota nation, the largest division of the Siouan stock, was made up of several groups whose customs and habitats illustrate the varying conditions of the Plains environment. These Indians were recent comers to the Mississippi region from the east;[224] the larger part of them crossed the Missouri and reached the Black Hills buffalo region between 1750 and 1775.[225] Their numbers, their wide range,[226] and their pugnacity (especially of the Teton) made them important figures in our border history.[227]

Linguistically, as well as geographically, there were three divisions of the Dakota:[228] the Santee, including the Mdewakanton, the Wahpeton, the Wahpekute and the Sisseton tribes; the Yankton, including the Yankton and the Yanktonai; and the Teton. The Santee are the eastern, and the Teton (with whom the Yankton are often grouped)[229] the western tribes. The seven tribes are said to have once been members[230] of a single tribe; and " while no

---

[223] 1915b, 827.

[224] Immediately, from the upper western Great Lakes region (Handbook, 1:376); originally, with the other Siouan tribes, from farther east (Mooney, 1894).

[225] Mooney, 1900, 157; Handbook, 1:376.

[226] During the historic period, almost all of South Dakota, the northwestern part of Nebraska and the southern half of Minnesota were claimed by the Dakota; and the western tribes wandered over even a wider territory.

[227] Most of the literature, and almost all of the early accounts of the culture of the Dakota concern the eastern tribes. Cf. Wissler, 1912, 3.

[228] Dorsey, J. O., 1891, 257–263; Williamson, 248. Cf. Carver, 37.

[229] See map of the Indians of the Plains, Wissler, 1920, 14.

[230] By some, gentes.

political organization has been known to exist within the
historic period of the whole Dakota nation, the traditional
alliance of the ' Seven Council-fires ' is perpetuated in the
common name Dakota, signifying allied, friendly." [231] The
Santee tilled the soil,[232] and from the economic point of view
should be classed with the semi-agricultural eastern Plains
Indians; the Yankton and Teton, however, were typical
Plains tribes.[233]

Morgan,[234] J. O. Dorsey,[235] and other early observers
thought they found a gentile organization or its traces
among all the Dakota. But this generalization does not
hold for the western tribes; if these once possessed exogamous paternal groups, their social organization was transformed by the change of habitat.[236] The band was the
unit. Concerning the eastern Dakota, however, recent
studies bear out the early accounts. According to Skinner,
" all three major bands of the Eastern Dakota were subdivided into exogamous patrilineal gentes, each of which
had its place in the tribal camp circle and each of which
had its own civil officers." [237]

THE TETON DAKOTA

The Teton, the largest division of the Dakota, were
described in 1794 as a " ferocious people, little civilized,
who wandered around constantly for food, filled with bar-
barous customs and manners. The vast prairies, which

---

[231] Dorsey, J. O., 1897, 221; Keating, 1:424. Cf. Walker, 72.

[232] At least during the historic period. But, " it is possible that
these Sioux obtained these things ¶corn, beans, etc.) from the
whites." Skinner, 1919, 167.

[233] Williamson, 248, 239. The Teton, however, have been credited
with attempts to cultivate maize. Cf. Wissler, 1920, 29–30.

[234] P. 154.

[235] 1891; 1897, 213. Cf. Radin, 184, 185.

[236] Walker, 73; Wissler, 1911, 2–5; Clark, 347; Handbook, 1:378.
Cf. Dodge, 85.

[237] 1919, 172.

they cross north of the Missouri, were presently stripped
of wild animals and they were obliged to come to hunt the
buffalo and wild cows on the banks of the Missouri and
even to cross over to the west bank for hunting." [238] Little
is known of their general culture.[239] Some observers credit
them with attempts to raise corn; but the early accounts
deny this.[240] The tribe was divided into seven bands.[241]

With the Teton, "the tendency was for the people to
scatter out in winter, but early in the spring the camp was
formed and its government organized." [242] As typical of
the tribe, we shall describe the government of the Oglala,
the dominant division of the Teton.

There were four bands of this subdivision, each with
slightly differing governments. In the Red Cloud band,[243]
for example, the governing body was the chiefs' society,[244]
" composing the majority of the efficient older men of forty
years or more. It elected its own members. Independent
of its organization, it elected seven chiefs [245] to govern the
people. These chiefs were elected for life. Since it was
customary for vacancies to be filled by the election of a

---

[238] Trudeau, 419.

[239] Wissler, 1912, 3.

[240] Wissler, 1920, 29, 30; Riggs, viii.

[241] Walker, 73.

[242] Wissler, 1912, 8. Cf. Walker, 73.

[243] Wissler, 7.

[244] Though started by succesful warriors about 20 generations
ago, according to one tradition, the chiefs' society was in the historic
period only a feasting and dancing association. Its members did
not participate in war parties. It was the highest and oldest order
of akicita societies, composed of men between 30 and 40 years of
age, who had won recognition in the tribe. Cf. ibid., 36–41.
" While it is claimed that the chiefs are not akicita, our data show
that they may exercise similar functions on occasion; but since
they are recognized as the governing body of the tribe this is not
inconsistent " (38).

[245] This number was not, however, a fixed one.

worthy son or relative, these offices were partially hereditary.[246]

" These seven chiefs did not actually participate in the daily government but delegated powers to younger or more virile men, by the appointment of four councilors to serve for life,[247] though they could resign at any time. These may or may not be members of the chiefs' society but the seven chiefs are not eligible to the office. . . . [They] are the supreme councilors and executives. They are charged with the general welfare; to see that good hunting is provided, healthful camp sites selected, etc. Thus, though theoretically deputies, these four men are the real power in the government."

The directors of the camp [the wakicun] were elected by the chiefs, often with the advice of the shirt wearers and the chiefs society. They served one year. " The wakicun are after all the true executives, the shirt men standing as councilors. A tipi was set up in the center of the camp circle as the office of the wakicun. . . . The shirt men as well as the seven chiefs had seats there as councilors. . . . "[248] The head akitcita, who served continuously during the season, were appointed by the executives.

" . . . It is clear that all the civil and economic affairs of the camp are in the hands of the wakicun. On all these matters, they are free to instruct and can enforce their orders through the akicita. They decide when to break camp, where to go and again select the new site. Hunting must be carried on when and as they direct. They also

---

[246] Cf. Walker, 74.

[247] These were known as the " shirt wearers " from their investiture garments.

[248] Wissler, 8. De Smet mentions councils of the Oglala. (1863, 43; 1905, 631). Councils of other Teton tribes are described or mentioned in De Smet, 1863, 44, 99; Mooney, 1896, 798; Catlin, 2:173; Lowie, 1913a, 137.

see that every person receives a fair share of meat and is provided with enough robes to make the winter endurable. They settle disputes, judge and compound crimes, and make rules to ensure proper decorum in camp. However, our informants felt their chief function to have been the regulation of the hunt, or the conservation of the food supply." [249]

Another division of the Oglala, the Kiaksai, had " the wakicun and their akicita but no shirt wearers. Instead of seven chiefs they had six who themselves exercised the functions of the four shirt men. There was no chiefs society, but all of the older men of the camp were considered as a general council with power to appoint six chiefs. Otherwise, the operation of the government was about the same as in the Red-cloud division." [250]

Among the instructions given the Oglala shaman was a survey of the tribal organization and government.[251] This included a description of the council.[252]

The council [253] of the camp is composed of men who are accepted as councilors because they customarily assemble in formal circle about the council fire to consider matters of common interest to the band. It usually consists of the chief and elderly men of good repute, knowledge and experience, though any renowned man may sit in the council, and if the council give heed to his speeches or ask his views upon matters they are considering, he thereby becomes a councilor. Any councilor may cease to be such by not sitting in the circle about the council fire. A shaman may taboo

---

[249] Wissler, 11. Cf. Walker, 75.

[250] Wissler, 1912, 11.

[251] Walker, 72–75.

[252] Ibid., 74, 75.

[253] The council acknowledged the chief. It could, also, debar an heir-apparent, depose the chief, and choose a new leader if a vacancy existed. The chief " may command the marshals to do anything and if the command accords with the laws and customs of the Oglala, or the edicts of the council, they should obey him, but they should judge the propriety of the command." Walker, 74. Cf. Densmore, 1918, 448 ff. for Teton Dakota council songs.

the councilorship for any member of the band. The duties of the council are to consider and decide upon all matters of common interest to the band; to issue such edicts as they see fit; to command the herald to make such proclamations as they desire; and to hear and decide upon appeals from the judgments of the marshals: A shaman can act only as adviser of the council. The council must appoint the herald and the marshals of the camp, but each councilor is subject to the discipline of the marshals in the same manner as are all other members of the band. The only perquisites of the councilorship are the honors of being a councilor. Any act of the council is accepted when it is not opposed by councilors who have a sufficient following of members to enforce their opposition.

Any member may represent any matter for the consideration of the council, except matter authorized by a shaman and may speak before the council relative to any matter it may have under consideration . . . A shaman may give advice relative to the standing of any member of a band or relative to the exemption of any member from the operation of any edict by the council and his advice should be heeded. He may taboo any one and relief from such taboo or ban may be had only by act of the council approved by a shaman.

When Trudeau asked the Tetons about the chieftainship, they replied that they " did not have one grand chief greater than all the others. That each man was chief in his own cabin." [254] The semi-hereditary office seems to be " of modern date; that is, since the Indians first became acquainted with the whites." [255] The tribal government of the Oglala was formerly vested, it is thought, in the wakicun. [256]

THE EASTERN DAKOTA

Even the three divisions of the eastern Dakota had varying cultures. [257] The Isanti and Wahpeton were almost of the woodland type in material culture, and yet they resembled the Plains tribes as well as the southern Siouans

[254] P. 420.
[255] Prescott, 2:182; Cf. Neil, 290 ff.
[256] Wissler, 11.
[257] Skinner, 1919, 174.

in social and political organization. Geographical conditions led to a greater similarity of the Sisseton to the Plains Indians.

The Sisseton were divided into nine gentile groups, the Wahpeton into six and the Isanti into six. " Each gens had its group of twenty wakicun or councilors who had a tent of their own. . . . For matters of tribal importance the councilors of all gentes got together. All the councilors had equal authority and each gens voted as a unit. There was a herald who announced their decisions. The chief's office was hereditary in later years, but formerly men achieved the honor through wisdom and prowess. Perhaps there were no chiefs before white advent. On all occasions except when in tribal council the ćhief had no authority over the councilors; in the tribal council he was supreme. Each chief had his own ' head soldier ' or akitcita,[258] who was his agent in all affairs, and who held office for life." [259]

One of Lowie's informants sketched the government of the Sisseton: [260]

" . . . His tribe was ordinarily under the chieftaincy of a single man with power to make treaties. . . . The office was for life and was usually inherited by the eldest son, but if the eldest son did not enjoy a good reputation the next oldest son was chosen. Under the chief there were four ministers, known as akitcita. . . . Of the four akitcita, one was of superior rank and took the leadership in inviting people to a council. He was known as . . . ' food distributor,' and filled his office as long as he lived. . . . All the akitcita were supposed to police the camp. If, for example, one tribesman had killed another, the akitcita tried to reconcile the relatives of the slain man and the murderer

---

[258] Lowie's data indicate four instead of one. The akitcita were individuals and not, as among the Teton, entiré societies who were chosen because of their bravery.

[259] Skinner, 173.

[260] 1913a, 132, 3.

by offering a gift of horses to the former. When an akitcita died, the chief appointed one of his sons, or in the absence of any sons, some other man to fill the vacancy.

" While these were the officers governing the tribe under normal conditions, there was a complete suspension of their authority for the time of the annual buffalo hunt. Just before this undertaking ten ' judges ' were selected in a tribal council, and these exercised supreme authority during the chase. They were chosen only for one particular hunt, and another set would be appointed the following year. All the ten were alike in rank, and were not necessarily elected for bravery. They remained in a central tipi . . . while the hunters were camped in a circle on any one site, and issued orders through a crier. . . . " [261]

The Wahpeton [262] were divided into three local groups, all presided over by a single chief. . . . The chief had two orderlies, or akitcita, appointed by himself, who carried his orders to other men. The akitcita never took the initiative themselves. . . .

" At the time of a buffalo hunt two lodges were set up close to each other in the center of the camp circle, each being occupied by one head man. These tipis were called *tiyotipi.* . . . In each there were twenty sticks. About forty councilors went round the camp. . . . Whenever they came to a man they wished to appoint as chief, they discharged their firearms and offered him one of the sticks. . . . Thus they went from lodge to lodge until twenty leaders had been selected. . . .

" The twenty leaders then discussed the hunt and selected an old herald who cried out that evening that the people should be ready to move the next morning. . . . The twenty head men took the lead." The two tiyotipi

---

[261] Cf. another account given by a native of the government of the Sisseton, Lowie, 134.

[262] Lowie, 134–135.

head men selected four akitcita. From the time the group got near the herd, " until the end of the actual hunt, all the officers previously mentioned had nothing more to say, and the supreme authority was vested in these four new akitcita."

A second description [263] lists only two Wahpeton bands, each with an hereditary chief. Under each chief, there were two soldiers, chosen by the whole people. " In case of any dispute in camp the akitcita were expected to settle it peaceably, though the chief himself might help. The akitcita were elected for life." Two special akitcita were appointed for the hunts.

THE MANDAN, HIDATSA, AND CROW INDIANS

The culture and social organization of these three tribes are studied together because of the close contacts which existed for a long time between them. The Mandan and Hidatsa represented, from an economic point of view, perhaps the most advanced tribes in their section of the Plains area.[264] They were very successful agriculturists, though they used the buffalo. Morgan appears to be mistaken in his assertion that the Hidatsa brought horticulture to the Mandan and the upper Missouri region; the contrary seems true.[265] The Crow separated not long ago from the Hidatsa, went westward, dropped agriculture, and became typical Plains Indians. Their culture was greatly differentiated from the parent tribe.

As Lowie says: [266]

The Hidatsa, while most closely related to the Crow, have been in close contact with the Mandan for so long a period that the cul-

263 Lowie, 136.

264 Will and Spinden, 128. Cf. Matthews, 18 ff. on the arts of the Village Indians.

265 P. 158. Cf. Will and Spinden, 117; Matthews, 12, 37.

266 1917, 3. Cf. Catlin, 1:185.

ture of all three tribes must be considered in conjunction. That is to say, it is impossible to acquire an accurate picture of Hidatsa life without taking into account, on the one hand, the persistence of old elements characteristic of the parent tribe before its division into Crow and Hidatsa, and, on the other hand, the influence exerted by the Mandan subsequently to the Crow separation.

THE MANDAN

" In point of general culture the Mandans were superior to any of their immediate neighbors, surpassing even the other sedentary people, the Hidatsa and Arikara." [267] These Indians lived in at least nine fixed villages on the Missouri near the Heart River.[268] Though agriculturists, about half their food was derived from the hunt.[269] In 1837 (that is, shortly after our first extended accounts of the tribe) an epidemic of smallpox killed all but 125 of them. A reconstruction of the social organization of the tribe is made increasingly difficult, therefore, because of its almost complete extinction.[270]

The Mandan seem to have been divided into two sorts of bands. " By the first method, like the Pawnee, they were known according to the old village from which they had originally come. Maximilian names at one time eight villages in describing the old habitations; in other places he says they had thirteen and gives the names for six more. This gives fourteen distinct village names. He says that the people were known by the names of the villages whence they originally came and Morgan mentions [271] eight of the names given, as the gens names. This

---

[267] Will and Spinden, 128. The Mandans are linguistically related most closely to the Winnebago. (Handbook, 1:796).

[268] Ibid., 91, 103 ff.

[269] Ibid., 117–120.

[270] Cf. Lowie, 1917, 3. Travellers and field workers discovered little about the political organization of the Mandan.

[271] P. 158.

is the only trace of a gens organization found." [272] Descent
was in the female line.[273] Chieftainship in these bands was
dependent on military prowess and wealth.[274]

The most eminent and distinguished warriors, who composed the Black Mouths or Soldier society,[275] ruled the
tribe. Maximilian said [276] they "form a kind of com-
mittee, which decides all the principal affairs, particularly
general undertakings, such as changes of places of abode,
buffalo hunting and the like. If the buffalo herds are in
the vicinity, they watch them and do not suffer them to
be disturbed by individuals, till a general chase can be
undertaken. If, during this time, any one fires at a wolf
or other animal, the soldiers take away his gun, ill-use and
sometimes beat him, to which he must submit; even the
chiefs are not spared on these occasions." At times,
judicial duties were exercised by the leaders of the
soldiers.[277]

The soldiers were but the most important of various
societies. "The second method of grouping into bands
followed the lines of the general plains division according
to age. . . . For the men there were six recognized bands.

---

272 Will and Spinden, 129.

273 Morgan, 158; Lowie, 1914, 75, 76. Cf. the contrary (erron-
eous) statement by Will and Spinden (131).

274 "If he wishes to gain reputation and a claim to distinction, it
is necessary that he should make presents . . . This and military
glory are, in the eyes of these men ,the greatest virtue." Maximilian, 23:322. Cf. Ibid., 321, 322, 350, 353. Much of our information concerning the government of the Mandans is worthless
because of the confusion caused by the creation and maintenance
of chiefs by the whites. Cf. Lewis and Clark, 1:164, where the
explorers tell about making chiefs. On the demoralizing effect of
European contacts upon the tribal structure of the Indians, see
La Flesche, 151.

275 They were also called the Brave Men's Society. Lowie, 1913b,
312–315.

276 23:293.

277 Lowie, 1913b, 314.

As men grew older they went from one band to the next. Each band or society had a limited membership, and a place in the band above was only obtained by purchase from a member who was ready to resign his place, and try to purchase a place in a band still higher up. . . . Each society had a chief who was in charge of all important affairs." [278] " All the higher classes may, at the same time, belong to the band of the soldiers. . . . It is, however, understood that all the members must be satisfied with the purchase." [279] The Mandan, or, perhaps, the Mandan and Hidatsa, were the originators of the system of age-graded societies out of previously ungraded societies [280]

THE HIDATSA

The Hidatsa [281] lived in villages near the Missouri and Knife Rivers in close contact with the Mandan and Arikara from some time before the historical period. Several hundred years ago, according to their traditions, they gave up a nomadic hunting life, settled on the Missouri and became farmers under the influence of the Mandan.[282] This settlement brought contacts which helped the culture of the tribe. " Economically, they were not merely buffalo-hunters but also hoe-agriculturists and in connection with this feature they inhabited, for a part of the year, settled villages of earth lodges." [283]

---

[278] Will and Spinden, 129.

[279] Maximilian, 23:293.

[280] Lowie, 1916, 951, 954.

[281] The tribe was known as the Gros Ventre of the Missouri, as distinguished from the Atsinas, the Gros Ventre of the Prairie. It was also called Minatree, from the Mandan name for it.

[282] Will and Spinden, 117; Henry, 284; Matthews, 37.

[283] Lowie, 1917, 87.

The tribe formerly lived in three villages,[284] which were independent of each other and which had distinct chiefs.[285] It was divided into seven exogamous clans,[286] grouped into moieties of three and four clans.[287] After the devastating epidemic of 1837, the survivors of the three villages united. Lowie has summarized our knowledge of the government of the Hidatsa: [288]

---

[284] Catlin, 1:185; Maximilian, 23:367; Lowie, 17–18.

[285] " In olden times, before the Crows left, there were three chiefs who controlled and regulated the camp." Clark, 194. Cf. Lowie, 17.

[286] Lowie, 19. The clan concept of the Hidatsa and Crow was a unique conception of the mother tribe and " beyond those traits involved in the definition of an exogamous mother-kin " shared no traits with that of other tribes. (Lowie, 89). But the relationship between the two tribes is close only as contrasted with neighboring tribes (90). Lowie's conclusions regarding this clan concept are interesting in view of the discussion of the priority of the maternal sib:

" The Crow and Hidatsa systems resemble each other in being founded on the exogamous clan with maternal descent, while all other tribes of the region that have been studied with reference to their social organization had either no definite social subdivisions at all or followed the rule of patrilineal descent. Here, however, the resemblance ends. While the clans of both tribes bear designations of the nickname type, this trait is too widely diffused to be significant, and there is no suggestion of a dual division, while the Hidatsa clans are assembled in two moieties . . . It thus appears that not only are the Crow and Hidatsa quite different from the surrounding Plains tribes of both the Siouan and other stocks, but even between the Crow and Hidatsa there are far-reaching differences. Accordingly, we cannot advance in any positive way the theory that their social systems are but differentiations from an older system that existed prior to their separation." Lowie, 1912a, 207.

[287] " The moieties had no marriage regulating function . . . Their functions were in part political. Whenever matters of tribal moment were to be debated, the grouping of men was based on the dual division." Lowie, 1917, 21.

[288] Lowie, 18, 19.

It is impossible to understand fully the political relations of the several villages prior to consolidation. We may reasonably assume that they formed uniformly friendly and autonomous groups corresponding to the local bands of nomadic Plains tribes.

The form of internal government in a village is likewise not clear. My principal informant introduced the concept of the "winter chief," whose term of office began in the fall, when the leaves turned yellow and expired at the melting of the snow. According to this witness a new winter village was built every year. The winter chief was a man associated with some medicine bundle, but as to the exact method of his selection no data were obtained . . . He was often responsible for the safety and welfare of the people. On the other hand, he was entitled to credit if the buffalo were abundant and if many enemies were killed . . . Sometimes there was no chief because the man chosen was unwilling to risk the responsibilities of the position. The ideal chief seems to have been a man of general benevolence who offered smoke to the old people and feasted the poor . . .

I neither discovered how the village was governed during the summer nor what was the position of the retired chief . . .

The power of policing the village was vested in the Black Mouth society, one of the age organizations . . . Their principal functions were twofold. They superintended the communal buffalo hunt so as to prevent the premature stampeding of the herd; and they attempted to remove any misunderstandings among fellow villagers.

Members of the Black Mouth society served as executive aids to the chief, when there was a chief. The society, as among the Mandan, was composed of middle-aged or elderly men, who were rich (and honorable) enough to purchase entrance.[289] Two of its leaders carried "raven-lances," which were emblems of authority in the camp as well as in the meetings of the organization.[290]

The Black Mouths acted as a police force. Whenever some difficulty arose in the tribe or between friendly tribes, this society tried to effect a reconciliation. At certain times they forbade people to go on the warpath.[291]

---

[289] Lowie, 1913b, 274.

[290] Ibid., 275, 279.

[291] Ibid, 277.

If an Hidatsa had killed another, the relatives of the slain man might plot revenge; but the Black Mouths would gather together property and offer it to the aggrieved people, fill a pipe for them to smoke, and by gentle words would conciliate them and cause them to give up projects of revenge.[292]

THE CROW

The separation of the Crow from the semi-agricultural Hidatsa took place about 1776; but, as Lowie indicates,[293] this conclusion rests, in a sense, entirely on linguistic grounds, since the cultures of the two tribes underwent considerable differentiation. Before the spread of white influence, the Crow were pure nomads,[294] ranging in and near the Rocky Mountains and the Yellowstone River. Leonard [295] (as early as 1834) found the tribe existing in two divisions, each headed by a chief; these groups were usually termed the Mountain and River Crow, according to their principal range.[296] There were no important cultural or linguistic differences between the two divisions.

Morgan's conclusions [297] in regard to the social organization of the tribe have stood the test of later investigations. The clan was the unit and the tribe was composed of " thirteen exogamous clans linked together into six loose phratries, most, if not all of which were non-exogam-

---

[292] Lowie, 1917, 19. Catlin gives a description of an Hidatsa council house and mentions meetings in it. (1:189, 195, 201).

[293] 1912a, 183.

[294] Lowie, 1922, 381.

[295] P. 255.

[296] " The Crow themselves recognize three local divisions of their tribe in former times . . . The first of these groups corresponds to the River Crow of some writers, and it was less closely affiliated with the two other divisions—often jointly designated as the Mountain Crow — than these were with each other." Lowie, 1912a, 183–84.

[297] P. 159.

ous." [298] Each clan had a head man who secured his place through martial prowess and success.[299] These leaders would often take their followers from the main encampment on hunting expeditions.[300] The camp circle was not regularly used by the Crow and the clans did not occupy definite places in it when it was employed.[301]

" There was no strong central power except at the time of a buffalo hunt or of some similar occasion calling for concerted effort. Those who had distinguished themselves in war by performing the four recognized deeds of valor [302] formed an aristocracy of ' chiefs ' and were highly esteemed. One of these acted as the camp chief, that is, he decided when and where the people were to camp." [303] The principal chief held office only as long as he had good fortune and kept his superiority in the number of deeds of valor.[304] During the sun dance the camp chief temporarily gave up his power to the owner of the doll, the chief ceremonial object.[305] Leonard gave [306] a scheme of social

[298] Lowie, 1917, 53. " . . . A considerable number of customs, including the joking relationship and the derivation of personal and nicknames, were dependent on the paternal clan, which is accordingly of very great importance in the social life of the tribe." Lowie, 1912a, 206. Cf. Goldenweiser, 1913.

[299] Lowie, 1917, 82.

[300] Lowie, 1912a, 186; Hayden, 394.

[301] Lowie, loc. cit.

[302] Cf. ibid., 230.

[303] Ibid., 228.

[304] " Long-Tree states that under some camp-chiefs a tribe had good luck, and then they would remain in office for a long time; but if the Crow had bad luck, they changed chiefs. Everything seems to point to the fact that the camp-chief had ordinarily strictly limited powers." Lowie, ibid., 229. " Whenever one person exceeds the existing chief in these deeds, he is installed into the office of chief of the nation, which he retains until some other ambitious, daring brave excels him." Leonard, 258. Cf. Bradley, 209.

[305] Lowie, 1915c, 50.

[306] P. 258.

stratification which included: common people, small brave, great brave, little chief, and great (camp) chief; but Lowie did not find two kinds of braves.[307]

A council of chiefs selected the camp chief, and ruled the united tribe when it met.[308] Only chiefs were entitled to debate matters of tribal interest.[309] One of the military societies was appointed by the camp chief every spring to serve as police.[310] The actions of the police could be vetoed by the chief.[311]

This rule by a council of chiefs is mentioned in legend.[312] De Smet,[313] Leonard,[314] and Beckwourth [315] have accounts of meetings.

THE ARIKARA

The Arikara, the southern of the three Village tribes, were Caddoan Indians, who once formed a single tribe with the Skidi Pawnee.[316] They settled in the upper Missouri Valley, coming from the southeast. They brought their agriculture with them and had considerable influence on the diffusion of culture in this region.[317] They hunted the

307 1912a, 228.

308 " Everything seems to point to the fact that the camp chief had ordinarily strictly limited powers and was simply the foremost among the chiefs." Lowie, ibid., 229. Of. Bradley, 209. It was, however, the council which, for example, declared war. Beckwourth describes (192) the punishment which came to those who disobeyed the council. " In their public buildings (council houses) all their national affairs are discussed at stated periods by the warriors and principal men." Leonard, 257.

309 Lowie, 229; Leonard, 259.

310 Leonard, 257; Beckwourth, 154.

311 Leonard, 258; Lowie, 229.

312 Belden, 206 ff.

313 1863, 158; 1905, 1037.

314 P. 263 ff.

315 Pp. 192, 221, and, especially, 224.

316 Dorsey, G. A. 1906, 8.

317 Lowie, 1912b.

buffalo in winter. Lewis and Clark found them living in three villages in 1804. War and disease forced them to abandon these in 1833, after which they lived with the combined Village tribes.

"Our knowledge of the general culture of the Arikara is exceedingly fragmentary."[318] The early observers noticed that their customs and political organization were somewhat like that of the other Pawnee tribes.[319] The tribe was "a loosely organized confederacy of sub-tribes, each of which had its separate village and distinctive name."[320] These village groups had their own head chiefs, but there appears to have been a head chief for all.[321] The chieftainship was, in part, hereditary.[322]

Brackenridge wrote concerning the government of the Arikara:[323]

Their government is oligarchical, but great respect is paid to popular opinion. It is utterly impossible to be a great man amongst them, without being a distinguished warrior; and though respect is paid to birth, it must be accompanied by other merit, to procure much influence . . . Their hunting is regulated by the warriors chosen for the occasion, who urge on such as are tardy, and repress, often with blows, those who would rush on too soon.

---

[318] Lowie, 1915a, 647.

[319] E. James, 17:153. Cf. Dunbar, 245: "In personal appearance, in tribal organization and government, in many of their social usages, and in language they are unmistakably Pawnees. The latter claim that since their separation the Arikaras have degenerated, and with some reason, for in many particulars they are decidedly inferior."

[320] Handbook, 1:86; Cf. Clark, 44.

[321] Lewis and Clark, 1:139–41. Cf. Trudeau, 459: "The many families of tribes of which these villages are composed, each having its own chief, proves a great obstacle to keeping harmony amongst them."

[322] Brackenridge, 111, 123; Bradbury, 174.

[323] Pp. 123–124. Cf. Lowie, 1915a, 656: The police duties of the Black Mouths (soldier society) are attributed to Mandan-Hidatsa influence.

The chiefs formed a council, which was, in a certain measure, responsive to the wishes of their followers. They sometimes called in the old men for advice.[324] This council regulated the intervillage affairs, especially warfare. Bradbury considered it, also, a sort of court, punishing intra-group murders with death, deputing the executioners.[325] The leading medicine man, who kept the sacred bundles so essential a part of Pawnee ritual, could call councils and other meetings, according to one tradition.[326]

THE PAWNEE

The Pawnee,[327] the leading Caddoan tribe, was a confederacy of four tribes, who lived in the Platte Valley of Nebraska: the Skidi, the Chaui, the Kitkehahki, and the Pitahauerat, known to the whites respectively as the Loups, the Grand, the Republican, and the Tapage Pawnees. These tribes and the Arikara, who are related to the Skidi, were probably immigrants from the southwest,[328] and there are undoubted traces of such a habitat in their customs and beliefs. The Skidi, who were the chief tribe in historic times, were once a single tribe with the Arikara; the other three tribes, with the Chaui at their head, were united.[329] All practiced agriculture,[330] the influence of

---

[324] Trudeau wrote that when he asked an Arikara chief to make peace with his neighbors, " he applauded my plan, but he said he must first call a meeting of the principal men of the nation, to impart to them our plan and obtain their approval." (467). Cf. Ashley, 71; Brackenbridge, 112, 118, 127; Bradbury, 120, 129; Dorsey, 1904c, 40, 86, 114, 119.

[325] P. 176.

[326] Dorsey, 1904c, 119.

[327] Grinnell, 1889; Dunbar; James; Dorsey, G. A., 1904b; 1906; 1907; A. C. Fletcher, in Handbook.

[328] Grinnell, 223; Dunbar, 251 ff.

[329] Dorsey, 1906, 8; 1904b, xiii.

[330] Dunbar, 276–7; Grinnell, 253; Dorsey, 1904b, xvii.

which can be seen throughout their ritualistic system.[331]
Hunting became more important after they acquired the
horse.

The social units of each of the tribes were villages or
bands.[332] The Skidi were composed of thirteen, the Pitahauerat of two, and the Chaui and Kitkehahki of one each.
" These villages, or bands, were the social unit, but seem-
ingly placed no rigid restrictions upon marriage. A man
got his place in a village through his mother. . . . the
villages were in principal endogamous." [333] Uniting the
villages was a ritualistic system based upon sacred
bundles.[334] Each group had its own bundles; while some
were common to the tribe. An asymmetrical dual division,
with important (shifting) functions, played a part in the
ceremonial and social organization.[335]

Our first complete account of the government of the
Pawnee was written by Dunbar over forty years ago: [336]

The government of each band was vested nominally in its
chiefs, these ranking as head chief, second chief, and so on. In
ordinary matters the head chief consulted his own pleasure in direct-
ing the affairs of the band. At other times he was assisted by a
council called for special deliberation . . Many of the chiefs used
their influence steadfastly for promoting the welfare of their people,
. . . and proving themselves in reality the fathers of their people.
Such chiefs exerted great power over their bands. On the other
hand a chief was sometimes only such in name, being surpassed in
actual influence by those of no recognized rank. The office itself
was hereditary, but authority could be gained only by acknowledged
personal accomplishments . . .

Besides their usual functions, chiefs were often called upon to
arbitrate in personal differences between members of their respective
bands. Their decision in such cases was accepted as final. The

---

331 Wissler, 1917b, 337 ff.
332 Murie, 549; Dorsey, 1904b, xviii.
333 Murie, 549.
334 Loc. cit.
335 Ibid., 642.
336 Pp. 260–262. Cf. Grinnell, 260, 261.

government of the tribe was exercised by the concerted action of the chiefs alone, or assisted by tribal council. Until recently the Xaui have held the precedence, their head chief outranking those of the other bands.

Councils of a band or tribe could be called by the head chief on his own motion, or at the prompting of another. If the matter to be brought under deliberation was of great consequence, or involved anything of secrecy, the council was appointed in a lodge, or at a place removed from immediate observation, and no one not personally entitled was admitted. In other cases any convenient place, indoors or out, might be named, and those not strictly privileged to sit in the council could, if disposed, attend as spectators. The right to participate in tribal or band councils was a much-coveted dignity. The call and time of assembling was duly published by the herald or crier of the chief . . .

The council on assembling, after the usual preliminary of smoking, was opened by the head chief, or by some one designated by him. After his will had thus been made krrown, the discussion was thrown open to all present as members; but great scrupulousness was observed that there should be no infraction of their rules of precedence and decorum. Rank, seniority and personal prestige were all carefully considered in determining the order in which each one should speak. . . . After the discussion of the matter in question was closed, the opinion of the council was gathered, not by any formal vote, but from the general tenor of the addresses that had been delivered in the course of the debate. The result was then made public through the herald.

Almost all our recent knowledge of the Pawnee concerns the Skidi, whose thirteen villages were federated under the bundle scheme. In this tribe, according to Murie,[337] " the governing body was a society of chiefs, twelve or more in number. It seems that in principle there was to be one chief for each village bundle, though as such, he had nothing to do with the bundle. . . . The chiefs were of equal rank and inherited their office. However, there was some selection, for the elderly men filled vacancies from those directly descended from chiefs. All the chiefs taken together constituted the tribal council of the Skidi.

---

[337] P. 554–556.

"The chiefs are, however, not the highest authority, that distinction belonging to the priests of the four main bundles. Their office is hereditary. . . . In rotation the four leading priests take over the responsibility of the welfare of the people for one year. . . . This chief priest is the highest authority; he is the source of final appeal,and to him all acts of the council of chiefs must be referred. . . .

". . . There is a chief for each village bundle . . . and he is theoretically at least the custodian, but there is another man in his village who is the keeper of the ritual, or the priest. He conducts the ceremonies. In the last resort he is superior to the chief, especially the priests of the calf-bundle and the four leading bundles.[338] . . . . While it is true that the chiefs are all of equal rank, the chief of the four-bundle village . . . sits at the head . . . and so is, the leading, or head, chief."

Elderly warriors were chosen by the chiefs to serve as aids and advisers.[339] There was one for each village. Each selected three assistants, who acted as village police, but who had nothing to do with the buffalo hunt.[340]

THE WICHITA

The Wichita lived in the region from the middle Arkansas to the Brazos Rivers until they were dispossessed by the Comanche, the Kiowa and the more or less settled Siouan tribes.[341] With them have been closely associated the Waco and the Tawakoni (which may be regarded as subtribes), and the affiliated Kichai.[342] All four groups were primarily agricultural, though they hunted the buffalo.[343]

---

[338] Cf. the myth, "The Chief and the Medicine Man Quarrel," Dorsey, 1904b, 185.

[339] Murie, 557.

[340] Cf. Lowie, 1915a, 664.

[341] Handbook, article, Wichita.

[342] Dorsey, G. A., 1904a, 1; Marcy, 1854, 78; 1866, 159; Handbook, articles, Wichita, Waco, Tawakoni, and Kichai.

[343] Cf. Clark, 403; Dorsey, 1904a, 4; Burnet, 240; Kendall, 1:141.

The tribe did not have a clan system.[344] The social organization of the four tribes was described by Dorsey: [345]

The basis . . . was that of the village, at the head of which was a chief and a sub-chief. Election to the chieftainship was never through heredity alone, it being necessary that the chief's son should show not only marked ability, but bravery and generalship equal to that of his father. It was possible, as the stories themselves show, for the youngest and meanest born boy of the village through exhibition of bravery to rise to the position of chieftainship. But more than bravery was necessary, for the aspirant to this high place must have won the love and respect of the members of his tribe by acts of generosity and kindness covering the entire period of his life.

The power of electing the chief was in the hands of the head warriors, who virtually controlled the village and could make or unmake a chief, as they wished.[346]

Next in rank to the chief was a leader, whose title was The-One-Who-Locates, and whose duty it was to be constantly on the lookout for better village sites. . . . Next in rank, were the medicine-men, who were also priests of certain ceremonies, one of their number being known as the ' crier ' or ' announcer.'

From the remaining inhabitants of the village were selected one or more known as ' servants'. Their duty was to do the bidding of the chiefs and of the medicine-men, especially in time of ceremonies. After years of apprenticeship they became medicine-men.

Of the remaining inhabitants of the village the basis of rank was that of prowess in war, and wealth.

THE CADDO

The Caddo, the principal southern representatives of the Caddoan stock, were agriculturists who once lived just outside the Plains area. They moved westward to the plains and became hunters as well as farmers. They lived

---

[344] Mooney, Handbook, 2:949.

[345] 1904a, 6, 7.

[346] Cf. statement of Mooney (Handbook, 2:949): " Their head chief . . . seems to be of more authority than is usual among the Plains tribes."

about the lower Red River of Louisiana, when first met by
the whites.[347]

Like its cognate tribes, it was divided into village groups,
which each had their chiefs, their priests and their ceremonies.   Chieftainship was hereditary.[348]   Descent was
maternal.   Dorsey's volume of Caddo traditions gives us
some information about the social organization of the tribe.
Their culture hero told them, according to their origin
myth,[349]

> it was very necessary that they should have one man abler and
> wiser than any other man among them ,to be their head man;
> that they should call him "chief"; that whatever the chief should
> command should be done by the people; that they should look upon
> him as a great father.   The unknown man told the people to return
> to their homes, hold a council among themselves and select a chief.

Councils of the chiefs, as well as tribal assemblies, are
mentioned in the traditions.[350]   As with the Pawnee, councils of animals and of men and animals are part of the
tribal lore.[351]

THE IOWA

With the Oto and the Missouri, an almost extinct tribe
associated with the Oto, the Iowa formed the Chiwere
group of Siouan Indians.   They were cultivators of the soil
at an early date, according to Dorsey and others.[352]

---

[347] Dorsey, G. A. 1905b, introduction; Mooney, 1896, 1092;
Fletcher, Handbook, articles, Caddo, Caddoan.

[348] Handbook, 1:181.

[349] Dorsey, 7.

[350] Dorsey, 14, 15, 86.   Lightning killed too many people.   The
chiefs held a council and decided to chase him away (30).   A chief
asserted in answer to a query, that he was away attending a council
(67, 68).   The chiefs held councils of war (54).

[351] Ibid., 14.

[352] Handbook, 1:613.   But this is disputed by Irvin and Hamilton (258), and Miner (18–19).

The tribe existed in nine or ten exogamous gentes, each with four sub-gentes.[353] Social stratification was especially marked, according to Skinner.[354] Sharp lines were drawn between the three generally endogamous classes: the hereditary chiefs and their families; the braves and their families; and the people at large.

Civil chieftainship was hereditary and was limited to the "eldest male lineal descendant of the four ancestors, the descendant of the eldest brother being paramount in each gens."[355] In the sub-gens the position went to the leading family. The tribal chief was the oldest representative of the bear gens in winter, and of the buffalo gens in summer: the leaders of the two divisions of the camp circle. The owners of the gens' war bundle and the leading braves conducted the military affairs of the tribe.[356]

The chiefs of the principal gens appointed a leader for the march, who performed various supervisory functions. Each chief had two soldiers attached to him. These enforced the decisions agreed upon.[357] The chiefs exercised great power in Iowa society, but councils of leading braves were held. Ordinarily, however, the chiefs formed a council to the head of the tribe.

THE OMAHA

"The tribal organization of the Omaha," according to Fletcher and La Flesche,[358] "was based on certain fundamental religious ideas, cosmic in significance." The dual division was clearly marked. The tribe existed in two divisions, which were mythically related: one represented

---

[353] Skinner, 1915, 683.
[354] Pp. 683–684.
[355] Ibid., 685.
[356] Ibid., 686.
[357] Ibid., 685.
[358] P. 134. Cf. Fletcher, 260.

the sky, the other the earth. These groups were subdivided into five bands or villages — or gens, which, however, were not political in nature.[359] This organization was
especially loose when they were in the buffalo country.[360]
The gens and sub-gens had no political or governing chiefs,
though members of the orders of chiefs often led them.[361]
The two principal chiefs, who were members of the governing council of seven chiefs, represented the two divisions,[362] and were merely those who could count the greatest
number of " deeds." [363]

Religious and political ideas were mingled in the theory
of the well-known Omaha council of Seven Chiefs, which
unified the tribe.[364] It was regarded as responsible to
spiritual powers for the welfare of the tribe and the direction of its political affairs. The Seven were chosen from
the highest order of chiefs,[365] membership in which was
limited. Warriors could join it — and only when there
occurred a vacancy in its small number — by the performance of certain acts which added to the welfare of the
tribe, such as the presentation of public gifts, especially
to the chiefs, making peace with an enemy, etc.

---

[359] The Omaha gens was characterized by the practice of a common rite, the title to which was inherited through the father.
Fletcher, 258; Fletcher and La Flesche, 195.

[360] Fletcher and La Flesche, 197. The tribal circle existed only
in summer. Dorsey, 283–84.

[361] Fletcher and La Flesche, 211.

[362] Ibid., 137; Fletcher, 263; Dorsey, 357.

[363] Fletcher and La Flesche, 208.

[364] " At meetings of the Council of Seven duty to the tribe was
ceremonially recognized by a formal mention of kinship terms between the members." Fletcher and La Flesche, 314.

[365] Originally, the Omaha chiefs inherited their positions. The
change to competitive membership came in recent times. Ibid., 202.
Dorsey, 361, 362. Places in the council were limited to certain
families in the seven groups of the gens and sub-gentes of the tribe
(Fletcher and La Flesche, 142, 185).

Five other persons could attend the meetings of the Council by virtue of their positions in this politico-religious scheme: the keepers of the Sacred Pole, of the Sacred Buffalo Hide, of the two Sacred Tribal Pipes and of the Sacred Tent of War. But none of these had any voice in the decisions.[366]

The duties of this deliberative body were all-embracing,[367] since the chiefs were the religious as well as the civil rulers of the tribe.[368] It maintained peace and order within the tribe;[369] kept its neighbors friendly; secured allies; designated the time for the spring planting[370] as well as for the annual summer hunts;[371] confirmed the appointment of the leader of the hunt;[372] appointed the soldiers who executed their orders, and, with the director, the special police for this occasion;[373] granted permission for the performance of rites; punished offenders who went out on unauthorized war parties;[374] and, if necessary, led the tribe against an enemy. On the hunt it was subordinate to the leader.[375]

To maintain peace was the principal aim of the council and its members were never, unless in extraordinary circumstances, leaders of war expeditions. In fact, one

[366] Fletcher and La Flesche, 208.

[367] Ibid., 209–211.

[368] Dorsey, 363.

[369] Cf. Fletcher and La Flesche, 213.

[370] Cf. Dorsey, 302.

[371] Cf. Fletcher and La Flesche, 276; Dorsey, 284; Edwin James, 1:201.

[372] Named by a certain sub-gens. Fletcher and La Flesche, 276; Dorsey, 286. While on the hunt the council, as with other Plains governing agencies, was subordinate to the leader, serving only in an advisory capacity. Fletcher and La Flesche, 209, 137.

[373] Fletcher and La Flesche, 279; Dorsey, 288; James, 1:207, 8.

[374] Fletcher and La Flesche, 404.

[375] Ibid., 209.

gens, which had charge of the war pipes of the tribe, was not given a place on the governing body.[376]

" There were no other governing chiefs in the tribe besides those of the Council. No gens had a chief possessing authority over it, nor was there any council of a gens, nor could a gens act by itself. . . . There was no tribal assembly or tribal council. All power for both decision and action was lodged in the Council of Seven." [377] The decisions of the council were regarded as the word of *Wakonda* [378] and required unanimity.[379] Meetings were conducted according to a fixed ceremonial procedure in which each member had a definite part and place.[380] They were called by the Hon'ga (leader) gens.[381]

It is not to be thought, however, that the council paid no heed to the wishes of the tribe. In deliberating on war, the leading men of the gens were usually heard, although the chiefs alone made the decisions, which were proclaimed to the people by a herald.[382] The authority of the council and the social order were safeguarded by the meting out to offenders of a punishment similar to, but more severe than the soldier-killings of other tribes.[383]

The origin of this powerful oligarchic body is told at some length in the sacred legend of the tribe. It was, according to our authorities,[384] " a development of earlier forms, rather than an arbitrary arrangement of the old men." All the accounts agree that it was devised to hold the people together.[385] The magico-religious sanction for

---

[376] Fletcher and La Flesche, 201.

[377] Ibid., 211.

[378] Ibid., 197, 208, 142.

[379] Fletcher and La Flesche, 208.

[380] Ibid., 208, 209; Dorsey, 358, 361, 363.

[381] Fletcher and La Flesche, 196.

[382] Ibid., 142.

[383] Ibid., 213.

[384] Ibid., 207

[385] Ibid., 201.

this departure was furnished by the two sacred pipes. "The credential of this authority of its creation and for the exercise of its function was the presence and ceremonial use of the two Sacred Tribal Pipes." [386]

In the Omaha Council of Seven Chiefs we view the act of the political wisdom of a particular group rather than the exemplification of a type.[387] It resulted from a peculiar situation which met the Omaha, who originally constituted one tribe with the Osage, Kansas, Ponca and Quapaw.[388] Maize and the buffalo, according to the sacred legend, came into their life before they reached the territory around the Missouri River where they settled. The evidence seems to indicate that their present form of government was established while they were in the region of the upper Mississippi on their way westward.[389]

THE OSAGE

From the earliest historical times the Osage lived near the Osage and the Little Osage Rivers in what is now Missouri. They differed but slightly in their mode of life from the Omaha and other semi-agricultural Siouan tribes who periodically left their villages to hunt the buffalo.[390] They continued to erect and live in the mat or bark covered habitations, which they and their cognates used in their earlier homes in the woodland to the east, long after they settled on the Osage.[391]

---

[386] Fletcher and La Flesche, 206.

[387] Ibid., 114: "Indeed, the Omaha seem to have been exempt to a remarkable degree from strong foreign control and to have developed their tribal organization in complete isolation."

[388] Fletcher, 255, 256. "The tribal organizations are similar and give evidence of having been modeled on a common plan, which may have been the plan of the parent organization from which these tribes split off" (Ibid., 256).

[389] Fletcher and La Flesche, 73–4.

[390] Lewis and Clark (T) 6:83, 84; Pike, Appendix II, 14; La Flesche, 43.

[391] Bushnell, 98.

Mythic conceptions underlay the Osage organization, as they did that of the Omaha, according to La Flesche.[392] The two great exogamous divisions denoted symbolic representations. The comparatively recent separation into three village groups or sub-tribes did not break up the earlier organization, which was ritualistic in its basis.[393] Three groups of seven gentes each made up the tribe, the Hon'ga, great division, symbolizing the earth, having fourteen gentes.

Pike, who was one of the first to write of the Osage, gave the following sketch of their government: [394]

> Their government is oligarchical, but still partakes of the nature of a republic, for although the power nominally is vested in a small number of chiefs, yet they never undertake any matter of importance without first assembling the warriors and proposing the subject in council, there to be discussed and decided on by a majority.
>
> Their chiefs are hereditary, in most instances, but yet there are many men who have risen to more influence than those of illustrious ancestry, by their activity and boldness in war. Although there is no regular code of laws, yet there is a tacit acknowledgement of the right, which some have to command on certain occasions; whilst others are bound to obey and even to submit to corporal punishment.

Two hereditary chiefs, representing the two great tribal divisions, ruled the tribe.[395] Their powers and duties were

---

[392] Pp. 48, 51, 59.

[393] Ibid., 45. Cf. Pike, Appendix II, 12.

[394] Appendix II, 9, 10.

[395] " Old men . . . familiar with the tribal traditions, say, in speaking of the office of chief,' When we were called to the great council we were given a place and the spokesmen of the council said to us . . . " Your office shall be one of kindliness, and within your house there shall be no anger, no hatred, you shall lead, and the people shall follow you in the paths of peace that they may live long and increase in numbers." The hereditary office then established was religious in character and was held through centuries in reverence by the people even with a superstitous awe." La Flesche, 151.

designated from the first, says the origin legend, and were primarily concerned with the maintenance of peace within the tribe,[396] and with the supervision of the hunt. The representative of the Sky people was given precedence in official rank.[397] Both chiefs selected the ten police who enforced their orders. In case an heir was disqualified, the soldiers in council elected the new leader.[398] Skinner noted the existence of social cleavage and class strata.[399]

The chiefs held councils both in the tribe and village.[400] Leading braves advised them and often determined the tribe's course of action. The chiefs gave some personal attention to private disputes.[401] Members of Long's expedition noticed that "their councils are very much distracted by the jealousies and intrigues of the principal chiefs and for want of energy and decision in the chiefs," [402] an observation also made by Pike and Hunter. Medicine men are said to have exerted influence upon the deliberations by their magical and occult performances.[403]

THE PONCA

Though linguistically closely related to the Omaha tribe, the Ponca, who lived on the Niobrara, differed from it in

---

[396] La Flesche, 54, 67.

[397] Ibid., 54.

[398] Ibid., 68; Dorsey, J. O., 1897, 235

[399] 1915, 684. The allegorical story of the origin of the tribe indicates three stages in the development of the political organization: 1. a military government under the domination of one gens; 2. a democratization of the military government; 3. the civil government. La Flesche, 65–68.

[400] Pike, Appendix II, 10, 11; Dorsey, J. O., 1897, 235; Edwin James, 2:245; Cf. Hunter, 310, 311, 320 ff.

[401] La Flesche, 67.

[402] James, 2:245.

[403] Pike, Appendix II, 10.

mode of life. They were primarily hunters.[404] " In material culture," says Skinner,[405] " the Ponca are of the Plains type with leanings toward the Central Algonkian whom they probably once resembled."

The tribe was divided into seven or eight paternal kinship groups,[406] each of which possessed, as among the Omaha, various exclusive duties.[407] It was one of the southwestern Sioux whose social organization was slightly stratified.[408]

The chiefs of the Ponca met in council to discuss the buffalo hunt,[409] select its leaders, etc. Fletcher and La Flesche give a narrative which tells of a council of chiefs called to adjudicate a blood feud.[410] While on the hunt the two temporary chiefs held councils with their police.[411]

In order to secure discipline, the two chiefs took the bravest men as wanuce. A waxobi pipe was kept in the tent, and when the soldiers and the chiefs were in council the head chief sat in the center of the circle . . . The council selected about forty youths who were known as good runners, or who possessed swift horses. The herald went around the camp, calling each by name and telling him that he was wanted at the soldiers' tent . . . If any one slipped out ahead (when the buffalo were found) he was reported to the

---

[404] Fletcher and La Flesche, 45: " There were no ceremonies in the Ponca tribe relative to the planting or care of maize. The Ponca are said to have obtained their maize more by barter than by cultivation." Cf. however, Skinner, 1915, 795: " Every year when the squaw corn was about a foot high " the chiefs held their council about the buffalo hunt.

[405] P. 779.

[406] Skinner (779) says seven; Dorsey, J. O. (1897, 228) and Fletcher and La Flesche, (51) give eight.

[407] Fletcher and La Flesche, 44 ff.

[408] Ibid., 61; Skinner, 684. The tribe had hereditary chiefs and others whose office was acquired through social and military merit.

[409] Skinner, 795.

[410] P. 50.

[411] The bravest warriors of some societies, but not the whole organizations were appointed by the chiefs to keep order in the camp and regulate the lines during the hunt. Skinner, 794–96.

chiefs who ordered the herald to call the soldiers to bring their weapons. They gathered, and were sent to the culprit's tent, where they dragged him out and beat him until he fell down, when they desisted.[412]

THE KANSAS

The Kansas were linguistically related to the Osage and the Quapaw.[413] Their agriculture was considerable,[414] though Lewis and Clark declared they spent eight months of the year away from their villages hunting on the upper Kansas and Arkansas Rivers.[415]

The social organization of the Kansas, according to Fletcher and La Flesche, was similar to that of their cognate tribes.[416] Pike noticed a close resemblance to the Osage.[417] The tribe existed in a dual division; these groups were composed of seven phratries of sixteen exogamous gentes.[418] Even while confined on an agency it kept its traditional grouping of villages or bands, each of which had a chief.[419]

Of the political organization of the tribe Skinner says: [420]

The tribe was governed by five hereditary chiefs whose offices were held in the five leading clans.[421] The five chiefs who first held office were doubtless elected by a common council of the people because of their bravery and wisdom, but the origin of these offices is now forgotten. Now the eldest son follows his father in office.

412 Skinner, 796–97.
413 Sibley MSS., quoted, Luttig, 36–37 notes; Pike, Appendix II, 17; Morehouse, 329; Dorsey, J.O., 1884, 1897; Handbook, art. Kansa.
414 Leonard, 60; Pike, loc. cit.; Handbook, 1:654.
415 Lewis and Clark (T.), 6:85; Lewis and Clark, 1:25–26.
416 Pp. 66–67.
417 Loc. cit. They were especially friendly with the Osage. Cf. Luttig, loc. cit.
418 Fletcher and La Flesche, loc. cit.; Dorsey, 1897, 230.
419 Spencer, 373; Morehouse, 353.
420 1915, 746.
421 Major George C. Sibley, who visited these Indians in 1811, reported that " they are governed by a chief and the influence of the oldest and most distinguished warriors " (cited, Luttig, 37n.).

In case a chief died and left no male issue, the office went to his brother or eldest daughter; hence, female chiefs were known. These civil chiefs, and those about to be mentioned, had no war powers whatever.

Besides the five hereditary chiefs, the people, in common council, could elect a chief and announce it to the world, after which he held office for life and his children became chiefs afterwards.[422] The chiefs themselves could also elect a commoner to join them without the consent of the people, if they felt the man was worthy and well qualified.

The three bands also had chiefs who were elected in common council,[423] at least in Choteau's time. A tribal chief was also so elected [424] and the other chiefs formed his council.[425]

Councils were called by the chief.[426] At times, the head chief performed certain duties of his office accompanied by " council warriors." [427] Leading braves, as well as chiefs, deliberated on proposals for war,[428] and the council represented the tribe in making peace[429] It also debated the subject of migration to new hunting grounds.[430]

---

[422] Say found a dozen of what he termed minor chieftians (291).

[423] There was a council house. Cf. E. James, 1:120: " The lodge, in which we reside, is larger than any other in the town, and being that of the grand chief, it serves as a council house for the nation."

[424] Cf. Spencer, 381.

[425] When Major Long's staff met the tribes' council of chiefs and principal men, there took place a dispute among the members concerning rank (James, 1:111–12, 120).

[426] Hunter, 42.

[427] Morehouse, 349. Maximilian was visited by the chief and six of his " council warriors."

[428] Ibid., 360 n. 28.

[429] Hunter, 40; Spencer, 380.

[430] Hunter, 31.

III

THE COUNCIL

The Indians of the Plains had little formal govern-government,[431] because they had little need of it. Continuous central authority was generally absent. There was much group and personal autonomy, and decisions of importance, as we have seen, were usually made by the headmen with the advice of a council.

Before the historic period little power seems to have been held by chiefs.[432] More often than not, chiefs (in a strict sense) did not exist, or else they were delegated limited powers (the Dakota, Crow, Comanche). Among some tribes (the Mandan, Hidatsa, Arapho) there was, it appears, only government by the leading men.

The council was the most important political institution among the Plains tribes.[433] Herbert Spencer thought the council originated in the gatherings of leading warriors, and that after the chieftainship became settled, the leader wished to conciliate the elders and share responsibility with them.[434] But the council, we find, is in the Plains area rather the pre-existing organization which may have created the chief, and was something more than a council of war. Almost without exception, the council was com-

---

[431] Wissler, 1921, v. The horse and the increase in warfare led to greater tribal unity and, occasionally, to the creation of a head chief where previously there was none.

[432] The Kiowa and Iowa, to mention two cases, seem to have been exceptions to this rule.

[433] In a rather sweeping generalization, Morgan long ago indicated the significance of the council among all our Indian tribes (116–17), though he was in error on important points. Cf. Waterman, 262–4, for a discussion of the tribal council in ancient Mexico, for as Bandelier proved, there was such a body with great powers among that people.

[434] Herbert Spencer " Principles of Sociology," New York (1909), 2:397 ff.

posed of the elders or the greatest warriors or both. In only a few instances (the well-known governing councils of the Omaha and the Cheyenne) were these bodies formal ruling agencies of long standing and highly developed procedure.

Age (and the wisdom which accompanies it) and military prowess are universally respected by primitive peoples. The elders are the custodians of tradition and customary law and they generally enforce these. Roughly speaking, this was true of all the Plains tribes. The police functions of the age societies sometimes centered this blanket power in a few individuals, yet hardly ever to the disadvantage of the elders.

There was much diversity in the political systems of this region. The councils were of many, varied kinds. The Iowa, the Omaha and the western Dakota, linguistically related, did not, however, possess the same political organization; [435] nor did the Arapaho and Cheyenne, Algonkian tribes who were neighbors on the plains. Yet we can describe the chief characteristics of the council; and the sketch would fit, more or less, most of the tribes.

The head chief was the leading member of the council. His power varied, according to his personal prestige and his mode of selection. He was hardly more than a respected leader of equals in some cases (Crow, Teton). Sub-chiefs, heads of the bands, the elders with a reputation for wisdom, and, at times, leading braves constituted its membership. The medicine men had influence (Oglala Teton), whether or not they were members. Women, children and

---

[435] "A grouping on the basis of social organization would certainly produce novel results, which would be somewhat similar but by no means coterminous with those arrived at if attention were concentrated exclusively on kinship terms . . . I have long felt that the Southern Siouan tribes should be linked with the central Alongkian rather than with the typical Plains people." Lowie, 1919, 77.

the young warriors were of course not admitted, nor were they usually heard.

A chief's lodge or that of the soldiers often served as a council house. Custom and deference to authority and rank marked both organization and procedure. Yet discussion was free and vigorous. Religious ideas and practices colored the deliberations. There were ceremonial approaches and ceremonial conduct. Feasts often preceded a meeting or served as the occasion for one.

Members met at the invitation of the chief, or when the occasion demanded it. Since the tribal government functioned primarily (and usually only) at the time of the tribal hunt, it was then that councils were held. But emergencies, such as the imminence of war, brought more frequent meetings. Where the council was a governing agency rather than a body advisory to a chief, deliberations were more numerous and regular. Some tribes held to the principle of unanimous consent, but this does not seem to have been universal.[436] Indeed, in many cases, there was nothing like balloting or voting; the consensus of opinion was merely taken.[437] Chiefs were often overruled or ignored or deposed. The results of deliberations were made known to the people by heralds or criers.

The council regulated all the tribal affairs or advised the chief concerning them.[438] Where chiefs were elected, it was the electing body; where they inherited their office it conferred office upon them. It settled the question of descent, where the candidates were of equal qualifications or where there was a dispute concerning the succession. The elders had some discretion even where the position was hereditary, since the eldest son might be passed over for a more capable member of the family. It declared war when there

---

[436] Cf. Catlin, 2:242.

[437] Cf. Grinnell, 1923; 1:339–40; Dunbar, 261; supra, 58.

[438] Cf. Wissler, 1911, 25; supra, 17; E. James, 2:373; Catlin, 2:239–40.

were such things as " official " declarations; and it made peace. It helped arrange the disposal of prisoners.

The council made plans for the tribal hunts, which were the most important tribal enterprises. Severe punishments were meted out to those who violated the communal spirit of these undertakings. Many tribes, in fact, recognized no crimes; i.e., offenses against the group, except infringements of the hunting regulations. After the hunt commenced, it was common for the council, together with the chiefs, to delegate all governing power to a small number of police (or a police society), who were dictators during the period of the chase. Such a vital matter as the migration of the tribe was left to the discretion of the elders, whose duty it was, also, to discuss and assert tribal and intra-tribal bounds and privileges.

Justice and judicial procedure [439] had not reached a high development among the Plains tribes. Difficulties were customarily settled by individuals and their blood-brothers. But the council, in time and among certain tribes, assumed judicial functions.[440] Among the Omaha, the council of seven chiefs punished deliberate murders by banishment and in other cases saw to it that composition was paid. The head men of the Blackfoot were expected to preserve peace in the tribe by settling the disputes of their band members.

The nature of Indian life implied that the council would have certain religious functions, as well as a magico-religious coloring. The cosmic conceptions which are inseparable from the social organization of the Omaha, its cognates and other Plains tribes, influenced its composition,[441] procedure and activities. The Omaha were not alone in declaring that the gods, who are the guardians of

---

[439] Cf. Lowie, 1920, 415–16.
[440] Cf. Catlin, 2:239–40; Du Lac, 67.
[441] Cf. Pond.

morality and the source of wisdom, gave authority to its acts and words. When calamities came — and these were regarded as essentially religious in nature — councils were held to make plans for material and spiritual remedies. The instructions of an Oglala shaman [442] sketch in detail the relations of a medicine man to the council in that tribe. The devout observances connected with meetings were in charge of the medicine men.

The tribal council was a great socializing force. It was a central ruling body for loosely connected bands and local groups. It emphasized the unity of the tribe and strove to increase its power and promote its welfare through various functions. It preceded the chief, existing as a body of ruling elders among tribes which had none. It supplemented the chief, acting as an advisory body which reflected the opinion of the band leaders and noted warriors. And, as we know, where a people have been allowed to fully develop their political organization, it remains, when the chief has become a king, or has disappeared, in the senate or upper house of their legislative body — in early times, as well as at present, the place for the elder statesmen.

---

[442] Supra, 43.

ABBREVIATIONS

The following abbreviations have been used to designate serial publications:

A.A.	American Anthropologist.
B.A.A.S.	Reports of the British Association for the Advancement of Science.
B.B.A.E.	Bulletin, Bureau of American Ethnology.
Cong.Am.	Proceedings, International Congress of Americanists.
J.A.F.L.	Journal of American Folk-Lore.
Kan.Coll.	Kansas Historical Society Collections.
M.A.A.A.	Memoirs, American Anthropological Association.
M.A.F.L.S.	Memoirs, American Folk-Lore Society.
Pa.A.M.	Anthropological Papers of the American Museum of Natural History.
R.B.A.E.	Annual Reports, Bureau of American Ethnology.
U.Cal.	University of California Publications in American Archaeology and Ethnology.

WORKS CITED

Ashley, W. H. 1918. The Ashley-Smith Explorations and the Discovery of a Central Route to the Pacific, 1822–1829. H. C. Dale, ed. Cleveland.

Bancroft, H. H. 1886. The Native Races, vol. 1. Works. San Francisco.

Beckwourth, J. P. 1856. The Life and Adventures of James P. Beckwourth. T. D. Bonner, ed. London.

Belden, G. P. 1874. The White Chief. Cincinnati.

Bent, Charles. Indian Tribes of New Mexico. In Schoolcraft, 1:242–246.

Boas, Franz. 1888. Preliminary note on the Indians of British Columbia. 58 B.A.A.S. 236–42.

1889. First general report on the Indians of British Columbia. 59 B.A.A.S., 801–893.

1918. Kutenai Tales. 59 B.B.A.E.

Brackenridge, H. 1904. Journal of a Voyage up the River Missouri. . . . R. G. Thwaites, ed. Cleveland.

Bradbury, John. . 1819. Travels in the Interior of America. London.

Bradley, J. H. 1917. Bradley Manuscript, Book F. 8 Montana, Historical Collections, 197–211.

Burnet, D. G. The Comanches and Other Tribes of Texas. In Schoolcraft, 1:229–241.

Bushnell, D. I. Jr. 1922. Villages of the Algonquian, Siouan and Caddoan Tribes West of the Mississippi. 77 B.B.AE.

Carver, Jonathan. 1796. Travels Through the Interior Parts of North America. Philadelphia.

Catlin, George. 1841. Illustrations of the Manners, Customs and Condition of the North American Indians. London.

Chamberlain, A. F. 1892. Report on the Kootenay Indians. 62 B.A.A.S., 549–615.

1905. The Kootenay Indians. Annual Archaeological Report, Ontario, 178–187.

Chamberlain, R. V. 1909. Some Plant Names of the Ute Indians. 11 A.A. n.s., 27–40.
1911. The Ethno-Botany of the Gosiute Indians of Utah. 2 M.A.A.A., pt. 5.

Clark, W. P. 1885. The Indian Sign Language. Philadelphia.

Densmore, Frances. 1918. Teton Sioux Music. 61 B.B.A.E.
1922. Northern Ute Music. 75 B.B.A.E.

Dodge, R. I. 1890. Our Wild Indians. Hartford.

Dorsey, G. A. 1904 a. The Mythology of the Wichita. Washington.
1904 b. Traditions of the Skidi Pawnee. 8 M.A.F.L.S.
1904 c. Traditions of the Arikara. Washington.
1905 a. The Cheyenne. Anthropological Papers of the Field Museum. Vol. 9. No. 1.
1905 b. Traditions of the Caddo. Washington.
1906. Pawnee Mythology. Washington.
1907. Social Organization of the Skidi Pawnee. 15 Cong. Am., Tome 2, 71–77.

Dorsey, J. O. 1884. Omaha Sociology. 3 R.B.A.E.
1891. The Social Organization of the Siouan Tribes. 4 J.A.F.L., 257–266.
1897. Siouan Sociology. 15 R.B.A.E., 213–244.

Du Lac, P. 1807. Travels Through the Two Louisianas . . . London.

Dunbar, J. B. 1880. The Pawnee Indians: Their History and Ethnology. 4 Magazine of American History, 241–281.

Fitzpatrick, Thomas. Tribes on the Sante Fe Trail. . . . in Schoolcraft, 1:258–264.

Fletcher, Alice C. 1906. Tribal Structure. A Study of the Omaha and Cognate Tribes. Putnam Anniversary Volume, 253–267. New York.
———— and La Flesche, Francis.
1911. The Omaha Tribe. 27 R.B.A.E.

Gilmore, M. R. 1919. Uses of Plants by the Indians of the Missouri River Region. 33 R.B.A.E., 43–153.

Goddard, P. E. 1907. Assimilation to Environment, as illustrated by Athapascan Peoples. 15 Cong. Am., Tome 1, 337–359.
1911. Jicarilla Apache Texts. 8 Pa.A.M.
1914. Dancing Societies of the Sarsi Indians. 11 Pa.A.M., 461–474.
1915. Sarsi Texts. 11 U. Cal. 189–277.

Goldenweiser, A. A. 1913. Remarks on the Social Organization of the Crow Indians. 15 A.A. n.s., 281–294.
1915. Social Organization of the American Indians, in Anthropology in North America, 350–378.

Grinnell, G. B. 1889. Pawnee Hero Stories and Folk Tales. New York.
1892. Blackfoot Lodge Tales. New York.
1900. The Indians of Today. New York.
1905. The Social Organization of the Cheyenne. 13 Cong. Am., 135–146.
1915. The Fighting Cheyenne. New York.
1918. Early Cheyenne Villages. 20 A.A. n.s., 359–380.
1923. The Cheyenne Indians. New Haven.

Hale, Horatio. 1846. U. S. Exploring Expedition. vol. 6. Eth-
    nography and Philology. Philadelphia.
    1885. Report on the Blackfoot Tribes. 55 B.A.A.S.,
    696–708.
    1887. Notes on the Report of Reverend E. F. Wilson. 57
    B.A.A.S., 197–200.
    1889. Remarks on North American Ethnology. 59
    B.A.A.S., 797–801.
Handbook. 1907–1910. Handbook of American Indians. F. W.
    Hodge ed. 30 B.B.A.E.
Hayden, F. V. 1862. Contributions to the Ethnography and Phil-
    ology of the Indian Tribes of the Missouri Valley. Philadelphia.
Henry, Alexander. 1897. New Light on the Early History of the
    Greater Northwest. The Manuscript Journals of Alexander
    Henry and of David Thompson. Elliot Coues ed. New York.
Hill-Tout, C. 1907. The Far West, The Home of the Salish and
    the Déné. London.
Holmes, W. H. 1919. Handbook of Aboriginal American Antiqui-
    ties. Part I. 60 B.B.A.E.
Hunter, J. D. 1823. Manners and Customs of Several Indian
    Tribes Located West of the Mississippi . . . Philadelphia.
Irvin, S. M. and Hamilton, William. History of the Iowa and Sac
    Tribes. In Schoolcraft, 3:259–276.
James, Edwin. 1823. An account of an Expedition from Pitts-
    burgh to the Rocky Mountains . . . Under the Command of
    Major Stephen Long. Philadelphia. Also Vol. 17, Early
    Western Travels, edited by R. G. Thwaites.
James, Thomas. 1917. Three Years Among the Indians and Mexi-
    cans. Waterloo, Iowa, 1846. ed., W. B. Douglas. St. Louis.
Johnston, A. Manners, Customs and History of the Root-Diggers
    and other California Tribes. In Schoolcraft, 4:221–226.
Jones, William. 1905. The Central Algonkin. Annual Archaeol-
    ogical Report, Ontario. 136–146.
Keating, W. H. 1824. Narrative of an Expedition to the Source of
    St. Peters River . . . Philadelphia.
Kendall, G. W. 1844. Narrative of the Texan Santa Fê Expedi-
    tion. London.
Kroeber, A. L. 1902. The Arapaho. 18 Bulletin, American
    Museum of Natural History, pt. 1.
    1907 a. The Ceremonial Organization of the Plains Indians
    of North America. 15 Cong. Am., Tome 2, 53–63.
    1907 b. Shoshonean Dialects of California. 4 U. Cal.,
    66–165.
    1908. Ethnology of the Gros Ventre. 1 Pa.A.M., 141–281.
    1917. The Tribes of the Pacific Coast of North America.
    19 Cong. Am., 385–401.
    1922 a. Introduction, American Indian Life.
    1922 b. Elements of Culture in Native California. 13 U.
    Cal.
    1923. American Culture and the Northwest Coast. 25
    A.A. n.s., 1–20.
La Flesche, F. 1921. The Osage Tribe. Pt. I. 36 R.B.A.E.
Lewis and Clark. 1815. Travels to the Source of the Missouri
    River and Across the American Continent . . . London..

Lewis and Clark (T.)   1904.   Original Journals of the Lewis and Clark Expedition.   Edited by R. G. Thwaites.   New York.

Leonard, Zenas.   1904.   Adventures of Zenas Leonard . . . Edited by W. F. Wagner.   Cleveland.

Lewis, A. B.   1906.   Tribes of the Columbia and the Coast of Washington and Oregon.   1 M.A.A.A., pt. 2.

Lowie, R. H.   1909a.   The Assiniboine.   4 Pa.A.M., 1–269.
    1909 b.   The Northern Shoshone.   2 Pa.A.M., 165–305.
    1912 a.   Social Life of the Crow Indians.   9 Pa.A.M., pt. 2.
    1912 b.   Some Problems in the Ethnology of the Crow and Village Indians.   14 A.A. n.s., 60–71.
    1913 a.   Dance Associations of the Eastern Dakota.   11 Pa.A.M., 101–142.
    1913 b.   Societies of the Crow, Hidatsa and Mandan Indians.   11 Pa.A.M., 143–358.
    1914.   Social Organization.   20 American Journal of Sociology, 68–97.
    1915 a.   Societies of the Arikara Indians.   11 Pa.A.M., 645–678.
    1915 b.   Dances and Societies of the Plains-Shoshone.   11 Pa.A.M., 803–835.
    1915 c.   Sun Dance of the Crow Indians.   16 Pa.A.M., 1–50.
    1916.   Plains Indian Age-Societies: Historical and Comparative Summary.   11 Pa.A.M., 877–1031.
    1917.   Notes on the Social Organizations and Customs of the Mandan, Hidatsa and Crow Indians.   21 Pa.A.M., 1–99.
    1919.   Review of Sapir, Time Perspective, etc.   21 A.A. n.s., 75–77.
    1920.   Primitive Society.   New York.
    1922.   Three Crow Tales, in American Indian Life, 17–44.
    1923.   Cultural Connections of California and Plateau Shoshonean Tribes.   20 U. Cal., 145–156.

Luttig, J. C.   1920.   Journal of a Fur-Trading Expedition on the Upper Missouri, 1812-1813, edited by Stella M. Drumm.   St. Louis.

M'Clintock, Walter.   1910.   The Old North Trail.   London.

M'Gee, W. J.   1897.   The Siouan Indians: A Preliminary Sketch.   15 R.B.A.E.

Mackenzie, Alexander.   1801.   Voyages from Montreal . . . . Through the Continent of North America.   London.

Maclean, John.   1896.   Canadian Savage Folk.   Toronto.

Marcy, R. B.   1866.   Thirty Years of Army Life on the Border.   New York.

————————, and A. B. McClellan.   1854.   The Exploration of the Red River of Louisiana.   Washington.

Matthews, Washington.   1877.   Ethnology and Philology of the Hidatsa.   Washington.

Maximilian, Price of Wied.   1905-6.   Travels in the Interior of North America.   Thwaites ed.   Vols. 22, 23, 24, Early Western Travels.   Cleveland.

Miner, W. H.   1911.   The Iowa.   Cedar Rapids.

Mooney, James. 1894. The Siouan Tribes of the East. 5 B.B.A.E.
    1896. The Ghost Dance Religion. . . . 14 R.B.A.E.
    1900. The Calendar History of the Kiowa Indians. 17
R.B.A.E., pt. 1.
    1907. The Cheyenne Indians. 1 M.A.A.A., pt. 6.
    1911. The Indian Ghost Dance. 16 Nebraska Historical
Collections, 169–186.
Morehouse, George P. 1908. History of the Kansa or Kaw Indians.
    10 Kan. Coll., 327–368.
Morgan, L. H. 1878. Ancient Society. New York.
Murie, J. R. 1914. Pawnee Indian Societies. 11 Pa.A.M., 543–644.
Neighbors, R. S. The Comanches. In Schoolcraft, 2:125–134.
Neil, E. D. 1850-1856. Dakota Land and Dakota Life. 1 Minne-
    sota Historical Collections, 254–294.
Paget, A. M. 1909. The People of the Plains. Toronto.
Parsons, E. S. ed. 1922. American Indian Life. New York.
Peeso, F. E. 1912. The Cree Indians. The Museum Journal
    (Philadelphia). Sept. 1912, 50–57.
Pike, Z. M. 1810. An Account of Expeditions to the Sources of
    the Mississippi . . . Philadelphia.
Pond, G. H. Power and Influence of Dacota Medicine Men. In
    Schoolcraft, 4:641–661.
Prescott, Philander. Contributions to the History, Customs and
    Opinions of the Dacota Tribe. In Schoolcraft, 2:168–199; 3:
    225–246; 4:59–72.
Radin, Paul. 1923. The Winnebago Tribe. 37 R.B.A.E.
Riggs, S. R. 1894. Dakota Grammar, Texts and Ethnography. vol.
    9. Contributions to North American Ethnography.
Sapir, E. 1916. Time Perspective in Aboriginal American Culture.
    Memoir 90 (Anthropological series, 13), Geological Survey of
    Canada.
Say, T. 1880. Part of his contribution to Edwin James' work is
    reprinted in 2 Kans. Coll., 280–301.
Schoolcraft, H. R. 1851-1857. Historical and Statistical Infor-
    mation Respecting the Historical Condition and Prospects of
    the Indian Tribes of the United States. Philadelphia.
Skinner, A. 1914 a. Political Organization, Cults and Ceremonies
    of the Plains-Ojibway and Plains-Cree Indians. 11 Pa.A.M.,
    475–542.
    1914 b. The Cultural Position of the Plains Ojibway. 16
A.A. n.s., 314–318.
    1914 c. Notes on the Plains Cree. 16 A.A. n.s., 68–87.
    1915. Societies of the Iowa, Kansas and Ponca Indians.
    11 Pa.A.M., 679–801.
    1919. A Sketch of Eastern Dakota Ethnology. 21 A.A.
n.s., 164–174.
Smet, P. J. de. 1863. Western Missions and Missionaries. New York.
    1905. Life, Letters and Travels. H. M. Chittenden and
A. F. Richardson, ed. New York.

Smith, H. I. 1906. A Vast Neglected Field for Archaeological Research. Boas Anniversary Volume, 367–72. New York.

Spencer, Joab. 1908. The Kaw or Kansas Indians. 10 Kan. Coll., 374 ff.

Speck, F. G. 1915. The Family Hunting Band as the Basis of Algonkin Social Organization. 17 A.A. n.s, 289–305.
1918. Kinship Terms and the Family Band Among the Northeastern Algonkins. 20 A.A. n.s., 143 ff.

Spier, L. 1921. The Sun Dance of the Plains Indians: Its Development and Diffusion. 16 Pa.A M., 451–522.

Spinden, H. J. 1908. The Nez Percé Indians. 2 M.A A S., 165–274.

Swanton, J. R. 1905. The Social Organization of American Tribes. 7 A.A. n.s., 663–673.
1906. A Reconstruction of the Theory of Social Organization, in Boas Anniversary Volume, 166–178.
1915. (With R. B. Dixon) Primitive American History, in Anthropology in North America, 5–41.

Trudeau, J. B. 1914. Journal of, Among the Arikara Indians in 1795. 7 South Dakota Historical Collections.

Walker, J. R. 1917. The Sun Dance and other Ceremonies of the Oglala Division of the Teton-Dakota. 16 Pa.A.M., 51–221.

Warren, W. 1885. History of the Ojibway. 5 Minnesota Historical Collections.

Waterman, T. T. 1917. Bandelier's Contribution to the Study of Ancient Mexican Social Organization. 12 U. Cal., 249–282.

Wilkes, Charles. 1845. The Narrative of the United States Exploring Expedition. . . . Philadelphia.

Will, G. F. and Spinden, H. J. 1906. The Mandans. Papers of the Peabody Museum. Vol. 3, No. 4.

Will, G. F. and Hyde, G. E. 1917. Corn Among the Indians of the Upper Missouri. St. Louis.

Williamson, T. S. Dacotas of the Mississippi. In Schoolcraft, 1:247–256.

Wilson, E. F. 1887. Report on the Blackfoot Tribes. 57 B.A.A.S., 183–200.
1888. Report on the Sarcee Indians. 59 B.A.A.S., 242–253.

Wilson, E. N. 1919. The White Indian Boy. Yonkers.

Wissler, Clark. 1905. The Blackfoot Indians. Annual Archaeological Report. Ontario. 162–177.
1907. Diffusion of Culture in the Plains of North America. 15 Cong. Am., Tome 2, 39–52.
1910. Material Culture of the Blackfoot Indians. 5 Pa. A.M., 1–175.
1911. Social Organization and Ritualistic Ceremonies of the Blackfoot Indians. 7 Pa.A.M., 1–63.
1912. Societies and Ceremonial Associations in the Oglala Division of the Teton-Dakota. 11 Pa.A.M., pt. 1.
1913 a. The North American Indians of the Plains. Popular Science Monthly, vol. 92.

1913 b. Societies and Dance Associations of the Blackfoot Indians. 11 Pa.A.M., 363–460.

1914. The Influence of the Horse in the Development of Plains Culture. 16 A.A. n.s., 1–25.

1916. General Introduction, Societies of the Plains Indians. 11 Pa A.M.

1917 a. The American Indian. New York.

1917 b. Comparative Study of Pawnee and Blackfoot Rituals. 19 Cong. Am., 335–339.

1920. North American Indians of the Plains. Am. Mus. Nat. Hist. Handbook Series, No. 1.

1921. General Introduction, Sun Dance of the Plains Indians. 16 Pa.A.M.

Wyeth, N. J. Indian Tribes of the Southern Pass of the Rocky Mountains. . . . In Schoolcraft, 1:204–229.

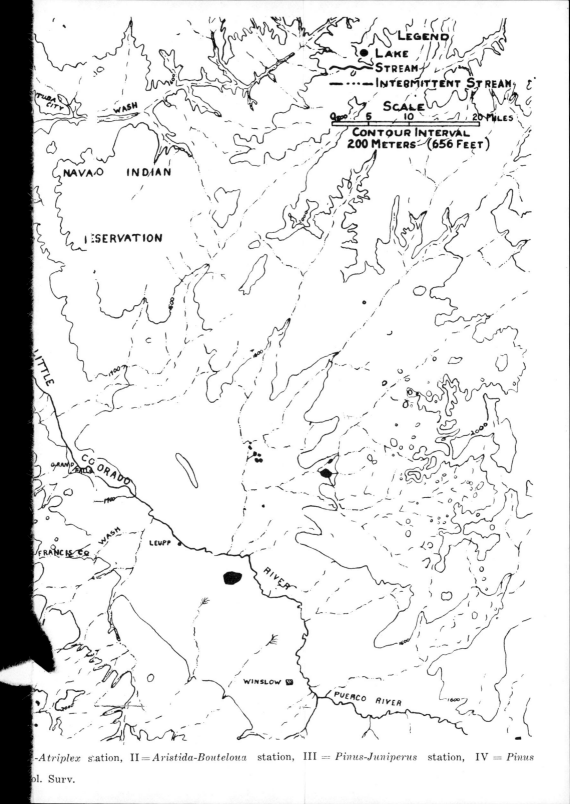

TUBA CITY

WASH

NAVAJO   INDIAN

RESERVATION

LITTLE

1700

400

2000

GRAND FALLS

COLORADO

1700

FRANCIS CO

WASH

LEUPP

RIVER

1800

WINSLOW

PUERCO RIVER

1600

-*Atriplex* station, II = *Aristida-Bouteloua* station, III = *Pinus-Juniperus* station, IV = *Pinus*

ol. Surv.

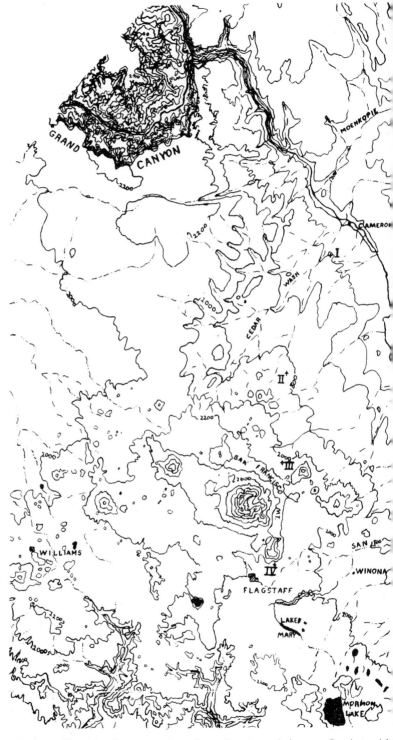

Fig. 1. Map showing a portion of northeastern Arizona. I = *Artemisia scopulorum* station.
Prepared from map of Arizona, Arizona Bur. of Mines and U. S. Ge